"Purdon and Clark are among the wor[ld's le]ading [experts in the understanding] and treatment of unwanted obsessional thoughts. In th[is book,] [they] describe powerful methods for conquering this problem, based on their own research as well as studies by other leading scientists. Although most self-help books on OCD include sections on dealing with unwanted thoughts, this excellent book provides the most thorough discussion of this topic that I've seen. Whether you have disturbing religious thoughts that you can't get rid of, irrational, unwanted, aggressive or sexual impulses, or other sorts of upsetting thoughts, this book is for you!"

> —Martin M. Antony, Ph.D., ABPP, director of the Anxiety
> Treatment and Research Centre at St. Joseph's Healthcare
> and professor in the Department of Psychiatry and
> Behavioural Neurosciences at McMaster University,
> both in Hamilton, Ontario

"Overcoming Obsessive Thoughts details powerful, proven, practical strategies that will enable people with obsessive-compulsive disorder to gain control over their obsessions and their lives. This book describes, in a clear and systematic way, a program for overcoming OCD. It provides a road map to a life without OCD."

> —Dennis Greenberger, Ph.D., coauthor of Mind Over
> Mood: Change How You Feel by Changing the
> Way You Think

"*Overcoming Obsessive Thoughts* is the best book on OCD that I have ever seen. This book helps you understand and help yourself with those intrusive thoughts and fantasies that plague your life. Clearly written, based on the latest research findings, and immensely helpful, this book will be a welcome guide to the millions of people who have obsessive-compulsive disorder. I will recommend this book to all of my patients with OCD. We are grateful to these two eminent psychologists for their insightful and practical guide."

> —*Robert L. Leahy, Ph.D., president of the International Association for Cognitive Psychotherapy, president-elect of the Academy of Cognitive Therapy, associate editor of* The Journal of Cognitive Psychotherapy, *professor of psychiatry at the Weill-Cornell University Medical College at New York Presbyterian Hospital, and director of the American Institute for Cognitive Therapy*

"This clearly written self-help book, from two acknowledged experts, is designed to assist sufferers overcome their unwanted, intrusive repugnant thoughts—obsessions. The nature and causes of obsessions are explained, followed by carefully constructed, systematic exercises. The exercises cover all three of the most common forms of obsessions—blasphemous, aggressive, and sexual—and users are encouraged to measure their progress by carrying out simple tests along the way. The tone of the book is kind, confident, hope-inducing, and encouraging. I expect that many sufferers will benefit from the book, and I strongly recommend it."

> —*S. J. Rachman, professor emeritus in the Department of Psychology at the University of British Columbia*

Overcoming Obsessive Thoughts

HOW
TO GAIN
CONTROL
OF YOUR
OCD

Christine Purdon, Ph.D., C.Psych.
David A. Clark, Ph.D., L.Psych.

New Harbinger Publications, Inc.

Distributed in Canada by Raincoast Books

Copyright © 2005 by Christine Purdon and David Clark
New Harbinger Publications, Inc.
5674 Shattuck Avenue
Oakland, CA 94609

Cover design by Amy Shoup; Acquired by Tesilya Hanauer;
Text design by Tracy Marie Carlson

Library of Congress Cataloging-in-Publication Data
Purdon, Christine.
   Overcoming obsessive thoughts : how to gain control of your OCD / Christine
Purdon and David A. Clark.
      p. cm.
   Includes bibliographical references.
   ISBN-10: 1-57224-381-3
   ISBN-13: 978-1-57224-381-1
   1. Cognitive therapy. 2. Obsessive-compulsive disorder. I. Clark, David A., 1954-
II. Title.
   RC489.C63P87 2005
   616.85'227—dc22

                              2005018929

New Harbinger Publications' website address: www.newharbinger.com

16   15   14

25   24   23   22   21   20   19   18

To Mary and William

—C.P.

To Natascha and Christina

—D.A.C.

Contents

CHAPTER 3

CHAPTER 4

CHAPTER 5

CHAPTER 6

CHAPTER 7

The Paradox of Mental Control   67

  * Introduction * Attention and Thoughts * Deliberate
Attempts to Control Thoughts * Research on Mental Control
* Why the Paradox? * Factors Influencing the Success of
Mental Control * Consequences of Failed Mental Control
* Effectiveness of Mental Control Strategies * Thwarting
the Paradox

CHAPTER 8

Overcoming Obsessions with Themes of Harm,   77
Violence, and Sex

  * Violent and Sexual Obsessions * What Are Your
Appraisals? * Thought-Action Fusion * Making Use of
This Information * Taking the Plunge: Exposure

CHAPTER 9

Religious Obsessions and Compulsions   93

  * Introduction * Religious Diversity * Does Religion
Cause OCD? * Religious Devotion: How Much Is Too Much?
* Faulty Appraisals and Beliefs * Challenging Appraisals
* Religious Counseling and OCD Treatment * Taking
the Plunge: Exposure

CHAPTER 10

Taking the Risk: Phasing Out Coping Strategies   117

  * Rationale for Phasing Out Coping Strategies * Taking It
One Step at a Time: The Exposure Ladder * Is It Dangerous
to Experience This Level of Distress? * Doing Exposure
Exercises * Keys to Successful Exposure * How Tos
of Exposure * Troubleshooting * Exposure Exercises
and Your Family * Quitting Cold Turkey

CHAPTER 11

Acknowledgments

We gratefully acknowledge the Social Sciences and Humanities Research Council of Canada, who awarded us a Standard Research Grant to conduct research on unwanted intrusive thoughts.

Overview of OCD

Obsessive-compulsive disorder (OCD) afflicts about 1 to 2 percent of the population, although many people may suffer from obsessions and compulsions that occur not quite frequently enough for them to be given that actual diagnosis (Clark 2004). About 90 percent of people with this anxiety disorder have both obsessions and compulsions, with approximately two-thirds reporting more than one obsession (Foa and Kozak 1995). Although it is very rare for a person to have a compulsion without an obsession, approximately 20 to 25 percent of people with OCD suffer from "obsessional rumination," which is the repeated occurrence of an obsession with no behavioral compulsion. Men and women are almost equally likely to have OCD, unless the OCD started in childhood, in which case it is more likely to occur in males. The usual age range during which people develop OCD is eighteen to twenty-four.

OCD has no specific cause. There is no known OCD gene, it is not associated with any abnormalities in the formation of the brain, and there are no specific features of background or personality that predict who gets it. People with OCD do appear to have more activity in areas of their brain that play a role in the ability to inhibit, or stop, behaviors than people without OCD, but it is unknown whether this is a cause of OCD or a symptom. Furthermore, these differences are reversed to the same degree with medication as with the kind of treatment we recommend in this book (Baxter et al. 1992). We do know that about 80 percent of people with OCD do *not* get better without help; that is, symptoms of OCD seldom disappear on their own.

WHO ARE WE?

We are clinical psychologists who have been researching and treating obsessions and compulsions for over a decade. We wrote this book because we are excited by new developments in our understanding of OCD and our ability to treat it. There are some new strategies that people can use to overcome their obsessions, and we feel that these strategies can be described in book form in a way that people can understand and use them. We find it highly gratifying to help people with OCD and watch as they regain their lives and live in freedom from the tyranny of obsessions and compulsions.

IS THIS BOOK FOR YOU?

This book is for you if you suffer from thoughts with violent, disgusting, or blasphemous themes that won't go away, even though you try very hard not to have them. People who have a formal diagnosis of OCD, as well as people who do not have that diagnosis but who experience obsessions, can benefit from this book. This is *not* the book for you if you have the kind of thoughts we are describing but find something pleasurable about them at some level. For example, if you experience sexual thoughts that are unwanted because they go against your morals, but the thoughts are pleasurable to you at some level (for example, they are sexually arousing), this book will not help you; you need to consult a mental-health professional in your area for assistance in coping with your thoughts.

WILL THIS BOOK HELP YOU?

The strategies we recommend in this book are strategies that have been shown by research to be effective in the treatment of obsessions and compulsions. Your success in using them will depend on several factors. The exercises will eventually require you to allow yourself to experience your obsession without doing a compulsion, or neutralizing or engaging in any avoidance or attempts to control the obsession. You will therefore be assuming some risk. For example, if you have a thought of harming someone while driving, we will be advising you to continue driving without doing your normal checking. If you have said or done something you think might have been a sin, we will be advising you not to atone for it or try to determine for certain whether or not it was a sin. If you have inappropriate sexual thoughts about someone, we will be advising you to continue to allow yourself to be around that person. To get better, you will need to be able to allow yourself to take these risks.

The risks you will be taking are educated, acceptable ones. If they weren't, everyone would have rituals and avoidance. We give the following advice to people, based on that given by Dr. Paul Salkovskis (1999), a leading OCD researcher and clinician: If you don't do anything about your obsessions and compulsions, we can pretty well guarantee that in six months you will have obsessions and compulsions to the same degree as you do now. If you follow the treatment and give it your best, you will be taking the tiny risk that something bad will happen, but we can pretty well guarantee that your obsessions and compulsions will be better than they are now. This may seem scary, but keep in mind that we will not be asking you to assume such risks until you have already done a lot of work to understand your OCD, and the risks truly feel acceptable to you; that is, much of this book is spent helping you get to the point where you are able to take these risks.

So, the answer to the question, "Will this book help me?" is, *yes*, it can help you!

WHAT'S AHEAD

Chapter 1 discusses the mainstream treatment of OCD. Chapter 2 presents a detailed description of obsessions and compulsions. Chapter 3 explains why obsessions and compulsions persist, even when people try very hard not to have the obsessions and do not want to do the compulsions. We then provide an overview of the treatment approach in this book and the logic behind it. Understanding the persistence of obsessions and compulsions and understanding the reasons behind the treatment procedure will empower you to make good decisions about managing your obsessions and compulsions. In chapters 4 and 5, we assist you in developing a good understanding of your own problem with obsessions and compulsions. Everyone experiences obsessions and compulsions differently, so it's important that you understand your own symptom profile.

Chapter 6 helps you identify potential obstacles to getting better and provides exercises to help you prepare for change. Chapter 7 provides information on how our minds work, which may alleviate concerns about your obsessions that actually end up making your OCD worse. Chapter 8 provides some case examples of people who experience obsessions with themes of harm or aggression and sex, and it offers exercises for coping with these particular types of obsessions. Chapter 9 deals specifically with religious and blasphemous obsessions. One of these two chapters may be more helpful to you than the other. Based on the types of obsessions you experience, you may choose to use one or both chapters. Chapter 10 presents the rationale for an essential component of treatment, which is exposure to your obsessions without engaging in any compulsive rituals, avoidance, neutralizing acts, or thought-control strategies. It offers detailed guidelines for setting up exposure exercises so that they are manageable for you. Finally, chapter 11 offers suggestions for maintaining your gains.

USING THIS BOOK

The approach to treatment taken in this book is known as *cognitive behavioral therapy* (CBT). CBT teaches a series of skills, each one building on the last. When people are highly motivated to overcome a problem, they often want to jump in and begin changing things as soon as possible. We know from experience that this approach isn't helpful in the long run. CBT is a process of skill development; first, you have to understand your problem and be able to identify problematic appraisals and coping strategies. Only then can you begin to introduce changes. If you skip the first chapters of this book, the later chapters will not be helpful. You need to do all the exercises outlined in chapters 1 through 7, in chapter 8 and/or chapter 9 (depending on your symptoms), and in chapter 10. We recommend that you purchase a workbook or journal to write the exercises in and that you keep these two books together.

Please resist the temptation to skip the early chapters. You will waste your money if you skip them. You also risk gaining nothing from this approach—not because the approach doesn't work but because you haven't developed the knowledge and skills necessary to benefit from it. Remember that your problem with obsessions and compulsions didn't start in a day, and it can't be treated in a day; if getting rid of OCD were that simple, you wouldn't have a problem with it.

PACING AND TIMING

We recommend that for chapters 1 through 3 and 5 through 7, you complete a chapter a week, in order. Chapter 4 involves establishing your symptom profile and will require two weeks. Chapters 8 and 9 focus on specific kinds of obsessive thoughts, so you can decide which ones you want to work on, depending on your own symptoms. These chapters require a minimum of two weeks each. Chapter 10 presents exercises for exposure to your obsessions. When you reach this part of the book, you should give yourself one week to come up with a list of increasingly difficult exercises that actually expose you to the obsession. It may take eight weeks because after that people do about one to two exercises per week, and there are usually about ten exercises to do; most people need about eight weeks to work through these exposure exercises.

It is best if you start each week by reading a chapter and then spending the rest of the week thinking about and doing the exercises. If you fail to apply the exercises in your daily life, then you will learn a lot about your obsessions, but nothing much will be likely to change. Reading the material in this book without doing the exercises is like hiring a fitness consultant and meeting with her or him once a week while doing none of the weight and cardio training that the trainer recommended; you would learn a lot about fitness, but your overall fitness level would not change.

We also recommend that you work through the book and on your OCD every week with no interruptions. If you are interrupted, be sure to review the earlier chapters and exercises before starting again.

CHAPTER I

Our Treatment Approach

MEDICATION AND OCD

If you are interested in taking medication for your obsessions and compulsions, you should definitely consult your family doctor. The treatment approach this workbook takes is compatible with medication use, and indeed the majority of people we have treated have been on medication during treatment. There is no magic pill that cures OCD, but medication can be helpful in reducing the frequency of and distress caused by obsessions. Medication appears to correct abnormal activity in the parts of the brain that play a role in the inhibition of behavior, or the parts of the brain that help people stop engaging in a specific behavior. However, not everyone benefits from medication, and the benefits of medication tend not to last once people stop taking it. The gains made in cognitive behavioral therapy usually last long past treatment stops, as it teaches skills that last a lifetime.

COGNITIVE BEHAVIORAL THERAPY AND OCD

The treatment approach used in this book is called *cognitive behavioral therapy* (CBT), which is considered the most successful psychological treatment of obsessional problems available. The main assumption of CBT is that thoughts and feelings are interconnected. Although you cannot change your feelings about things, you can examine your thoughts about things and make sure that you have a balanced view of them. If your view of situations is unbalanced, then your emotional reaction will be unbalanced (exaggerated or inappropriate). For example, many people experience obsessional thoughts just like the kind you experience, but they are not bothered by them. The reason is that those people do not interpret such thoughts to be meaningful or to be signaling harm or danger or to be something that requires action on their part. Thus, they can easily dismiss them.

SAME THOUGHT, DIFFERENT REACTION

Neema has a thought of swerving into the next lane while driving. She thinks, "What an odd thought for someone like me to have! I'm not the kind of person who would harm anyone." But Ravi, having the same thought, thinks, "Oh my gosh, why did I have that thought? Maybe I am a murderer at heart! What if I act on it? I can't have this thought again because what if having it makes me do it? I am a terrible person for having this thought. I don't really want to drive if I'm in danger of harming people." Neema is calm about the thought whereas Ravi is anxious and fearful about it. Whereas Neema is likely to continue on with her daily activities without any concerns about the thought, Ravi is likely to become increasingly concerned about having it. He may sift through all his prior experiences, looking for information that matches the idea that he may be murderous at heart. The more he does this, the less confident he becomes that he is not murderous. The more he thinks about the thought, the more likely he is to think about it when driving. This will begin to confirm his worst expectations about what the thought could mean. Ravi may then begin to avoid driving or to try to neutralize the thought by thinking a "good" thought or by some other strategy. Avoidance of the thought keeps Ravi from experiencing his obsession and from risking acting on the thought, and thinking a "good" thought helps relieve the distress he feels. Thus, Ravi will use these strategies more and more often.

THE DIFFERENCE IS IN THE INTERPRETATION

As you can see, the difference between Neema and Ravi was in their understanding of what it meant to have that thought. It's clear from research that Neema's understanding is accurate whereas Ravi's understanding is actually based on incorrect information about thoughts and thought processes. For example, even the most conscientious, pious, caring people can have thoughts of a violent nature that they would never ever act upon; there are numerous examples from history of highly religious people experiencing blasphemous thoughts or religious doubt. Furthermore, a person's true personality is not revealed in the occurrence of a single type of thought. Thus, having the thought by no means implies that Ravi is a murderer at heart.

Ravi is also the kind of person who feels that he shouldn't do something if there is a perceived risk of harm, no matter how small that risk. This is typical of people with obsessions and compulsions; they are much more likely to organize their lives to prevent all possible harm, even when the probability of that harm is close to zero. People without obsessions and compulsions will take acceptable risks. For example, Neema wouldn't say that she knew, 100 percent for certain, that she would never act on the thought, but she believes that the possibility of acting on the thought is pretty close to zero. Thus, Neema has no fear of continuing to drive.

WHAT DOES CBT DO?

CBT focuses on what you believe the obsessional thought means (your cognitive appraisal of the thought) and your behavioral response to the thought (that is, your use of avoidance, compulsions, neutralizing acts, or thought-control strategies). As you begin to understand that the thought might not mean what you think it means, your emotional response to the obsession becomes less intense, as does your need to perform a compulsion, neutralizing act, avoidance, or thought control. For example, if you realize that having a thought about a violent act does not mean you must have murderous qualities in your personality, you will fear the thought less. If you realize that your distress will decrease even if you don't do the compulsion, the compulsion will become unnecessary.

THE BEHAVIORAL PART

A major component of CBT for obsessions and compulsions is known as *exposure with response prevention*. This procedure involves exposing you to the obsession while prohibiting compulsions, neutralizing, avoidance, and thought-control strategies. This is a very powerful component of treatment.

When you experience your obsession, you feel bad in some way, and when you engage in compulsions or neutralizing acts, or avoid aspects of the situation that make you feel worse, you end up feeling better. It makes total sense that you do this, but terminating exposure to the obsession has a number of negative effects. First, it is clear from research that trying to get rid of a thought makes people much more sensitive to thought cues, and inevitable failures in thought control make people even more upset. Second, you never have the chance to realize that your bad feelings will go away even if you don't do the compulsion or neutralizing act. We know from extensive research over four decades that the bad feelings associated with obsessions go away on their own; the compulsion or neutralizing act is not necessary. Actually, it is true that almost all emotions go away on their own, even positive ones. Think of a time when you felt really joyful about something (your partner accepted your offer of marriage, or you passed a major qualifying exam). Were you as joyful one hour after hearing the news as you were three minutes after hearing the news? Third, when you use compulsions, neutralizing, avoidance, and thought control in response to your obsessions, you never get a chance to learn that your obsession may not be as dangerous as you think; your negative assumptions about the meaning of the obsession are never tested.

Consider the example of Stefan, who is as afraid of spiders as people with OCD are of their obsessions. Suppose Stefan finds himself in a room full of spiders and cannot get out. It is likely that Stefan's discomfort would shoot up off the scale. But would it stay there? That is, would Stefan's anxiety be as high one hour later as it was immediately upon being thrown into the room? What about two hours later? As Stefan remains in the room, he has the opportunity to learn new things about spiders that he has never learned before, because he has always fled when he sees them. For example, he has the chance to notice that spiders actually avoid large, moving objects like himself, and move away from him rather than scurrying up his legs. Ultimately, Stefan realizes that although being around spiders is not pleasant, it is not objectively dangerous; even the deadly black widow stays to itself and only poses a threat if it is actually touched. But if Stefan never stays around spiders, he never gets a chance to learn anything new about them. The same is true of your obsessions; the more you avoid, the less you know about them.

CHAPTER 2

Do You Have Obsessions and Compulsions?

SOME FACES OF OCD

Mario is a forty-three-year-old financial planner with two teenage daughters and a solid marriage that has just celebrated its twenty-second anniversary. He is a conscientious and hardworking university graduate who volunteers for a number of worthy community causes, is well-liked by neighbors and friends, and is admired for his determination and well-balanced approach to work, family, and community. And yet, Mario's day is filled with unwanted thoughts of violence and aggression toward others; thoughts of kicking a pregnant woman who passes him on the street, of punching a colleague in the mouth for no apparent reason, or lunging toward his wife with the knife he is using to cut up vegetables. These unexpected and unwanted intrusive thoughts are extremely upsetting for Mario because they are totally against his character. After all, he is a fine, outstanding family man with strong moral values who is polite and gentle toward others. But here he is, plagued by violent and repulsive thoughts and images.

Cara is a twenty-four-year-old mother of a four-year-old boy. She is a proud, loving parent who wants to provide the very best for her son. But shortly after arriving home with the infant, Cara began having thoughts or doubts about whether she might sexually abuse the child. While changing his diaper or bathing him, she wondered if she felt sexually aroused. This doubt became so frequent and troubling that she avoided bathing or changing her son and relied on her husband or visiting friends to do so. Her days were fraught with high anxiety and fear.

Anke is a fifty-two-year-old clerical worker who grew up in a strict fundamentalist Christian home, and her faith has continued to be a sustaining force in her life. She is a committed Christian and an active member of her local church. Her single desire is to live a life fully committed to Christ. And yet, for twenty years, Anke has been tormented by blasphemous thoughts and profanity that pop into her mind when she reads the Bible, prays, or listens to a sermon. She has sought repeated pastoral counseling for these terrible intrusions. She has prayed earnestly that the thoughts be taken from her, and she has even participated in an exorcism, convinced that she is being tormented by Satan, or even worse, demon possessed. These awful sacrilegious thoughts and images have become so intense that Anke wonders if there is any hope for her. Possibly she is doomed to Hell for her terrible sin.

Although these three individuals struggle with very different unwanted thoughts, images, or impulses, they all suffer from obsessive-compulsive disorder. This chapter provides a detailed description of obsessions and compulsions and then helps you determine whether you have thoughts and behaviors that might apply.

WHAT ARE OBSESSIONS?

Obsessions can come in three forms:

- words in your head, including doubts, such as "what if . . . ?" "did I . . . ?" "was that . . . ?"

- images, like a sudden picture in your mind

- impulses, or sudden urges to do something

Obsessions intrude suddenly into your mind and are unwanted, inappropriate, and distressing. Once an obsession occurs, it captures your attention, and it is very difficult to think of anything else. Even if you are able to distract yourself from the obsession, the relief is only momentary because obsessions occur again and again. Obsessions tend to involve ideas or content that is inconsistent with your personality or moral values, ideals, and goals.

The word "obsession" is often used to describe a passion, enthusiasm, or preoccupation with something (with a hobby, a celebrity, or a romantic partner, as in "he was obsessed with trains" or "she was obsessed with him"). The word as we use it is not about a passion or preoccupation or enthusiasm. Instead, it refers to unwanted, unwelcome, recurring thoughts that happen against your will and that are about unpleasant topics. When people's obsessive thinking is excessive—that is, they spend more than an hour over the course of a day experiencing or thinking about the obsession—and/or compulsive and neutralizing acts take up more than an hour over the course of a day, they are considered to have obsessive-compulsive disorder.

REPUGNANT OBSESSIONS

Obsessions have many different themes. This book focuses on obsessions that are known as *repugnant obsessions*. "Repugnant" means disgusting. The kinds of obsessions we are addressing in this book are obsessions that have a violent or harmful theme, a sexual theme, or a religious theme.

Those with a violent or harmful theme fall into these categories:

- images of doing something horrible to a loved one (throwing your baby off of a balcony; stabbing your grandchildren)

- urges to harm a loved one (urge to push a loved one off of a bridge; urge to stab a loved one)

- doubts as to whether you have accidentally harmed someone ("Did I run over someone back there but not notice it?" "Was the pot I used to cook dinner truly clean before I used it?")

Sexual obsessions fall into these categories:

- thoughts or images of engaging in a sexual act that you find personally disgusting (images of touching a child sexually; images of engaging in a sexual act that goes against your sexual orientation and repulses you)

- urges to engage in an exploitative and/or personally disgusting sexual act (urge to touch women on the street inappropriately; urge to make a sexually crude comment to someone)

- doubts about your sexuality, about whether or not you are a pervert or a child molester ("Did I become sexually aroused when I hugged that child?" "Did I linger on that TV station because the show featured children?" "Did I become sexually aroused by seeing other naked men in the dressing room?")

Obsessions with religious themes fall into these categories:

- thoughts or images of engaging in a sacrilegious act and/or of displeasing God (images of a religious figure engaging in a sinful or blasphemous act; ideas such as "I am condemned to Hell" or "The spirit of God has left me")

- impulses (urge to curse God; urge to say something blasphemous during a religious ceremony or while praying)

- general doubts ("Did I put my own desires before God?" "Did I sin but forget to repent?" "Is God showing me a sign?" "What if my actions or decisions bring punishment from God upon my loved ones?" "Did I praise God enough in my prayers?")

■   doubts that reflect scrupulosity, or extreme rigor and thoroughness, in following religious principles ("Was I completely truthful in telling my friend exactly what was on my mind?" "Could I have been misunderstood because I didn't tell that story correctly?" "Am I assured salvation?")

More detailed examples and discussions of thoughts with harm/ aggression and religious obsessions are presented in chapters 8 and 9, respectively.

The specific content of an obsession is unique to the individual, but most obsessions can be categorized under a few common themes. Rasmussen and Eisen (1998) studied the content of obsessions in over 1,000 individuals with OCD. They found that concerns about contamination and excessive doubts about actions or decisions were the most common. However, 31 percent of people reported having obsessions involving harm, aggression, or injury, 24 percent reported sexual obsessions, and 10 percent reported having religious or blas-phemous obsessions. Other types of obsessions included the need for symmetry or exactness, obsessions about health, and the hoarding of possessions.

FOCUS EXERCISE 2.1:
IDENTIFYING YOUR POSSIBLE OBSESSIONS

In your notebook, list any unwanted thoughts, images, or impulses that enter your mind repeatedly, are upsetting, and are very difficult to prevent or dismiss. Don't be too concerned right now about whether these are true obsessions or some other form of distressing thought. You will evaluate each of these thoughts for their "obsessional quality" later.

ARE YOUR THOUGHTS OBSESSIONS?

Obsessions are not the only type of unwanted and distressing thoughts that people struggle against. Most of us have worries, ruminations, preoccupations, daydreams, and so on that can have an impact on our emotional state. How can we know whether a recurring, unwanted, distressing thought is an obsession or some other form of negative thought? This section covers the critical defining characteristics of obsessions that you can use to evaluate whether the distressing thoughts and images you listed in Focus Exercise 2.1 can be considered an obsession or not. These five core features of obsessions are discussed in greater detail in Clark (2004) and are based on the criteria for diagnosing OCD in the *Diagnostic and Statistical Manual of Mental Disorders* (American Psychiatric Association 2000):

- **They have an intrusive quality.** Obsessional thoughts, images, or impulses appear in the mind quite suddenly and against the will. They are not intentional.

- **They are unwanted.** Obsessional thoughts cause considerable distress and so are wholly unwanted.

- **They involve resistance.** Most people with OCD struggle against the obsession, trying very hard to suppress, dismiss, or prevent the obsession from taking over. They also try to cope with the obsession by avoiding situations that trigger it or by performing a compulsive ritual or neutralizing strategy to reduce the distress it creates.

- **They are uncontrollable.** Individuals with OCD often report that they feel they have lost control over their obsessions and that they may be losing control of their mind.

- **They seem uncharacteristic.** The content of obsessions often goes against people's core values, moral standards, or personality. This feature of obsessions is called *ego-dystonic*. Ego refers to the self, so in this case the obsession is entirely contrary to your self-concept, the type of person you are, or the way you behave.

FOCUS EXERCISE 2.2:
ARE YOUR THOUGHTS OBSESSIONS?

Evaluate the unwanted thoughts you listed in Focus Exercise 2.1, rating them on a scale of 0 to 4.

Characteristics of Obsessions	Not at all	Slight	Moderate	Severe	Extreme
1. To what extent does the thought enter your mind against your will?	0	1	2	3	4
2. How upset or distressed are you by the thought?	0	1	2	3	4
3. How hard do you try to resist this thought?	0	1	2	3	4
4. To what extent are your efforts to control the thought unsuccessful?	0	1	2	3	4
5. To what extent does the thought go against your values, personality, and goals?	0	1	2	3	4

If you responded to most of these questions with a 3 or 4, then it is quite possible you are experiencing an obsessional thought. Whether the obsession is mild, moderate, or severe can only be determined by psychological testing and a clinical interview by a qualified mental-health professional.

"NORMAL" OBSESSIONS

Obsessional thoughts do not just happen to people who have OCD. There is mounting evidence that obsessional thoughts are quite common in the general population. Researchers in the United States,

Britain, Korea, and Canada have shown that 80 to 90 percent of people report unwanted intrusive thoughts with content that is identical to that of obsessions. This should come as no surprise. Research by psychologist Dr. Eric Klinger (1996) indicates that the average person has about 4,000 distinct thoughts in a sixteen-hour day. Approximately 13 percent of these thoughts are spontaneous, occurring without any intended purpose. Individuals reported that many of these thoughts were quite out of character, even shocking. Thus, the average person experiences approximately 520 spontaneous intrusive thoughts each and every day.

The following table presents data from our own research on university students, showing the percentage of students who reported aggressive, sexual, or religious intrusive thoughts (Byers, Purdon, and Clark 1998; Purdon and Clark 1993).

Percentage of university students who report different types of unwanted intrusive thoughts of aggression or sex and religion		
Obsessional Content	**Percent of Students**	
	Men	**Women**
Hurting a family member	50	42
Hurting strangers	48	18
Holding up a bank	32	8
Indecently exposing yourself	24	14
Sexual act that is against your religious values	38	24
Engaging in a "disgusting" act of intercourse	31	26
Sex with a child or minor	19	7
Forcing another adult to have sex with you	38	22

We have focused on aggressive, sexual, and religious intrusive thoughts because these obsessions are the primary focus of the book. What this research shows is that many, many people without an obsessional problem have exactly the same types of unwanted thoughts as people with OCD.

So what's the difference between these "normal" obsessions and the obsessions in OCD? The main one is that people with OCD report many more obsessions, and their obsessions are more intense, distressing, and difficult to control. As you will see in the next chapter, there are a number of psychological processes that operate to turn normal obsessions into excessive, problematic obsessions. The good news is that if you have engaged in some process that turned occasional unwanted intrusive thoughts into persistent obsessions, then you can be taught ways to reverse this process and turn your obsessions back into occasional unwanted intrusions.

CAN OBSESSIONS TURN UGLY?

One of the most frequent concerns expressed by individuals with OCD is that their obsessional thinking might actually come true. People worry that they may snap and act on their thoughts. If they did act on them, however, jails would be filled with people suffering from OCD who had given in to their thoughts. In fact, very few people with OCD ever break the law or act on their obsessions. Based on our clinical experience, we believe that people with OCD probably have a lower rate of criminal behavior than the general population. There are a number of reasons why individuals with OCD do not act on their obsessions. First, obsessions cause considerable anxiety and distress and are not gratifying at any level. This is not the case for thoughts that precede or occur during violent or exploitative acts. Dr. William Marshall, a psychologist who has spent decades treating sex offenders, notes that sex offenders find their deviant sexual and aggressive thoughts pleasurable, at least at some level, even if they do not want to be sex offenders or pedophiles (Marshall and Langton, forthcoming).

Second, there is more to committing an act of violence or exploitation than simply having thoughts about it. You may have unwanted repugnant thoughts involving molesting a child, but to be disinhibited enough to actually commit such a crime, you must be willing to view your own sexual desires as more important than preserving the innocence of a child, and/or you must be able to talk yourself into believing that sexual contact with children is somehow not harmful to them. Our experience with people who have OCD is that they are not preoccupied with finding ways of harming others; instead, they are preoccupied with how to preserve the safety, health, and happiness of others. So, to act on the obsession would require that strongly entrenched personality traits, moral values, and ideal standards be overridden, which is something that does not happen spontaneously.

SCRUPULOSITY: A SPECIAL CASE OF RELIGIOUS OBSESSIONS

This section is meant for people who are bothered by frequent and distressing thoughts of a religious nature. If you do not suffer from thoughts with a religious theme, you may want to skip to the section on compulsions and neutralizing.

It is normal for people of faith to aspire to live their faith on a daily basis, bringing spirituality and religious precepts to bear on their actions regularly throughout the day. When do religious thoughts cross the line from being healthy expressions of faith to being excessive and problematic thoughts characteristic of OCD? To help answer this question, consider the concept of *scrupulosity*. According to Dr. Joseph Ciarrocchi (1995), a clinical psychologist and associate professor of pastoral counseling, a person with scrupulosity is one who has an overly sensitive conscience and who might see personal sin where there is none. The scrupulous person has an unhealthy fear and insecurity that hampers religious adjustment so that he or she "sees evil where there is no evil, serious sin where there is no sin, and obligation where there is no obligation" (Weisner and Riffel 1960, p. 314). Weisner and Riffel note that judgment can become so skewed that a scrupulous person will consider something as being very important when in reality it is minor or trivial. For example, someone who is scrupulous might be preoccupied with the concern that he or she spilled a drop of holy water on the floor, or with ensuring that every part of his or her body is absolutely clean prior to offering prayers, or with repeating particular words or minor sections of a prayer in order to get the wording exact.

Scrupulous individuals often recognize that their concerns about sin and punishment are excessive and possibly even illogical. They also realize that others in their faith community are not hampered to the same degree by such concerns. And yet, scrupulosity as a form of OCD leads to such unrelenting doubt, guilt, and anxiety, the person is left thinking that something is wrong. Such thoughts might include, "When I looked at that attractive woman, did I have a lustful thought?" "Was I fully concentrating when I said that prayer?" "Am I putting God first in all my decisions?" "Did God really forgive me?" or "Did I confess every sinful thought and desire to the priest?"

Scrupulous individuals are often in a struggle to attain a level of moral perfection where even the smallest deviation from adherence to a religious practice or the commission of a moral error or misjudgment cannot be tolerated. This striving for perfection is often combined with an intolerance of uncertainty. Scrupulous people must be certain that they have no unconfessed sin, that God has truly forgiven them, and that they are not condemned to Hell. Together, these beliefs and intense negative emotions imprison them with religious obsessions and compulsions into a never-ending struggle for moral and spiritual perfection.

If you are a person of faith, you may be wondering whether you suffer from religious obsessions or scrupulosity. What is the difference between strong religious faith and the OCD disorder called scrupulosity? This is an important question because we do not want to falsely diagnosis the religious person or, on the other hand, to ignore those suffering from religious obsessions and compulsions.

FOCUS EXERCISE 2.3: SCRUPULOSITY VS. RELIGIOSITY

Psychiatrist Dr. David Greenberg (1984) discussed a number of criteria that can be used to distinguish emotional (clinical) scrupulosity, a form of OCD, from strong religious devotion.

The following is a list of features for problematic scrupulosity (religious obsessions). Read each statement and decide how much the statement describes you. Place an X along the scale below each statement to indicate how much it applies to you.

1. I am mainly concerned about one or two areas of faith or morality.

> *Not at* ⊢————————————————————⊣ *Exactly*
> *all like me*   *like me*

2. My concerns focus on religious/moral issues that are rather minor or trivial according to the spiritual guides in my faith community.

> *Not at* ⊢————————————————————⊣ *Exactly*
> *all like me*   *like me*

3. My fears about faith/morality prevent me from engaging in the religious practices valued in my believing group.

> *Not at* ⊢————————————————————⊣ *Exactly*
> *all like me*   *like me*

4. I try to resist my scrupulous behavior but to no avail.

> *Not at* ⊢————————————————————⊣ *Exactly*
> *all like me*   *like me*

5. I also have other symptoms of OCD.

> *Not at* ⊢————————————————————⊣ *Exactly*
> *all like me*   *like me*

6. My concerns and fears about morality occupy much of my day, interfering with my ability to work and relate to others.

> *Not at* ⊢————————————————————⊣ *Exactly*
> *all like me*   *like me*

7. I am greatly distressed by fear of sin and God's punishment.

> *Not at* ⊢————————————————————⊣ *Exactly*
> *all like me*   *like me*

If you felt that most of these statements were relevant for you, then you might be struggling with problematic scrupulosity. Whereas these religious obsessions and compulsions cause a great deal of personal distress, accepted forms of religious devotion bring personal fulfillment and contentment, and enhance, rather than impair, a person's daily functioning and relations with friends and family.

The first four statements in Focus Exercise 2.3 refer specifically to scrupulosity. People with religious obsessions usually focus on one or two moral issues, often to the exclusion of more important aspects of their faith. For example, a person may be preoccupied with whether he or she has sinned by having an impure sexual thought whereas he or she may act quite unkind, even nasty, toward friends or family. As well, the focus of religious obsessions is often on quite trivial matters that are of no concern to most others in the person's faith community. Often the scrupulous behavior will interfere with the performance of religious practices that are valued by the person's faith group. For example, a person may stop going to church or refuse to receive communion because it triggers distressing thoughts of sin and God's punishment. In addition, individuals with scrupulous behavior may unsuccessfully try to resist their religious compulsions. This differs from the religiously devout person who, far from trying to resist his or her religious behavior, takes great interest and delight in faith practices and observances. In the final analysis, OCD with a religious focus is quite different from normal forms of religious devotion and practice. If you suffer from scrupulosity and/or religious obsessions, you will want to pay special attention to chapter 9.

COMPULSIONS AND NEUTRALIZING

When people have obsessions, they typically feel discomfort, anxiety, disgust, or a sense of feeling "not just right." When people have obsessions, they try to get rid of them in some way and/or reduce the unpleasant feelings by performing some kind of act. When the act is repeated exactly the same way every time, it is called a *compulsion*. Compulsions are acts that people feel compelled to perform; that is, they don't feel they have a choice but to perform them. When the goal is to "undo" the obsession or atone in some way and the act can vary in how it is done, it is called a *neutralizing act*. Rasmussen and Eisen (1998) found that 61 percent of their sample of individuals with OCD had checking compulsions, 50 percent had washing compulsions, 36 percent had counting rituals, 34 percent needed to ask or confess (seek reassurance), 28 percent showed symmetry and precision behaviors, and 18 percent showed hoarding. Compulsions can be actual behaviors you engage in (washing your hands) or mental acts (thinking a "good" thought).

EXAMPLES OF COMPULSIONS AND NEUTRALIZING

Repugnant obsessions most often give rise to these compulsions and neutralizing strategies:

- "undoing" or "neutralizing" a "bad" thought by thinking a "good" or "safe" thought (forming and holding an image of a loved one being safe or happy in response to an aggressive thought, urge, or image; forming and holding a pure image in response to a blasphemous thought, urge, or image)

- engaging in some form of ritual to prevent harm the thought might cause (washing your hands; counting to a "lucky" or "holy" number, or repeating an action a specific number of times; correctly reciting a specific passage from scripture or a religious text)

A very common type of compulsive act in response to repugnant obsessions is checking (Abramowitz et al. 2003). Checking can take various forms, including the following:

- checking that if you have caused harm, you have been forgiven or the consequences are not as catastrophic as feared (repeatedly contacting your spiritual advisor to confess sins and receive absolution/forgiveness; confessing actions to the police to determine if the actions are criminal)

- checking for yourself that harm hasn't occurred (scouring the newspaper and television for reports of hit-and-run accidents; closely monitoring your body for signs of sexual arousal; checking that the knives are safely in the knife block; reviewing all your previous activities in the day to ensure that there has been no sinful act)

- seeking reassurance from others that harm hasn't occurred (asking a child every few minutes if he/she is feeling okay; asking a close friend or spouse whether he/she thinks you are gay or perverted; repeatedly contacting your spiritual advisor to determine if a specific act constitutes a sin)

- rationalization, or mental self-reassurance (examining homosexual pornography on the Internet and attempting to determine if arousal is greater to it than to heterosexual pornography; scouring religious texts to determine if a particular action or thought was sinful; determining how well characteristics of known pedophiles match your own characteristics; reading religious scripture for a passage that assures salvation; reciting a prayer of confession after every sinful thought)

Often the goal of reassurance is to obtain 100 percent certainty as to whether the obsession is true. Some individuals report that they would feel relief even if they were to find out that the obsession is true because they would then be certain as to how to proceed. For example, if they knew for sure they were a pedophile, they could make arrangements for someone else to care for their child, without feeling guilty or conflicted.

A response qualifies as a compulsion or a neutralizing act if it has these four characteristics:

- *The response is intentional, repetitive, and excessive.* Compulsive responses and neutralizing acts are intentional and repetitive actions. Although they may become automatic or habitual, over time they are done deliberately (unlike obsessions, which do not occur deliberately). The acts are also excessive in their frequency. You do not just ask once for reassurance, or just pray once, but rather repeat the act many times throughout the day.

- **You feel an urge to do it.** The person with OCD often feels a very strong internal pressure to perform the compulsion ritual or neutralizing act. Although people with OCD may initially resist giving in, the pressure mounts and often they end up performing it. Over time, you may stop resisting the urge and give in to it right away. When the compulsion or neutralizing act is completed to satisfaction, the pressure to continue performing the ritual subsides until the next occurrence of the obsession, or until you doubt whether the act has indeed been performed properly.

- **You feel a loss of control.** People with OCD can feel enslaved to compulsive rituals and/or neutralizing acts, as if they have no control. They feel that the need to perform the compulsion or neutralizing ritual controls them. Some people spend most of their waking hours repeating compulsions and neutralizing acts, at the expense of important activities.

- **The response is performed to cope with negative feelings or consequences.** The person with OCD performs compulsions to reduce the distress associated with the obsession and performs neutralizing acts to "undo" the potential harm that having the obsession might cause, or to in some way atone for having had the obsession. Compulsions and neutralizing acts often lead to a reduction in distress and/or a sense of relief (the loved one is no longer in danger, the sin of the obsession has been atoned for). Even if compulsions or neutralizing acts don't lead to a reduction in distress or afford much relief, people with OCD believe their distress would be significantly greater if they did nothing in response to their obsessions; hence the compulsion or neutralizing act is perceived as having at least prevented worse distress.

FOCUS EXERCISE 2.4: DO YOU USE COMPULSIONS OR NEUTRALIZING?

Using the following questions and rating scale, evaluate whether any of your responses to unwanted, distressing, intrusive thoughts would qualify as a compulsion or neutralizing strategy. In your workbook, write down the mental or physical actions you perform to cope with your obsessions. Use a scale of 0 to 4 to evaluate your responses.

Characteristics of Compulsions and Neutralizing	Not at all	Slight	Moderate	Severe	Extreme
1. To what extent do you tend to engage in the same response over and over?	0	1	2	3	4
2. How strong is the urge to perform the response?	0	1	2	3	4
3. To what extent do you feel you have lost control over the response?	0	1	2	3	4
4. To what extent do you engage in the response to feel better or to prevent a possible negative outcome?	0	1	2	3	4

If your response to most of these questions was a 3 or 4, the response may qualify as a compulsion or neutralizing strategy.

THOUGHT CONTROL AND AVOIDANCE

We know that people with OCD use a variety of other strategies to manage obsessions, in addition to compulsions and neutralizing acts. Freeston and Ladouceur (1997) found that individuals with OCD use compulsions only 25 to 33 percent of the time when they have an obsession, using a variety of other coping strategies instead, such as thought-control strategies, self-punishment, and avoidance. Purdon, Rowa, and Antony (working paper) found that people with OCD often use thought-control strategies to get rid of an obsession before the compulsive act or neutralizing strategy becomes necessary. The following list offers a brief description of some control strategies that people use to manage their obsessions:

- **Avoidance.** These are attempts to reduce the frequency of obsessions by staying clear of situations, people, objects, colors, and so on that might trigger the unwanted intrusive thoughts, or make the distress over the thoughts worse (for example, avoiding children, or at least avoiding being in a room alone with a child). People with religious obsessions may avoid secular entertainment or even attending religious ceremonies.

- **Trying to convince yourself that the thought is unimportant.** Attempts to convince yourself that the obsessional thought is not significant or important. An example would be telling yourself "Everything is going to be okay, this thought doesn't mean anything."

- **Thought-Stopping.** Shouting "stop" to yourself, mentally or out loud.

- **Self-Criticism.** Making critical, disparaging remarks to yourself about having repugnant obsessional thoughts or images.

- **Distraction.** Attempts to shift your attention from the obsession by doing something or thinking about something else.

- **Thought replacement.** Attempts to replace the obsession with another thought (Clark 2004).

Even though people with OCD use a variety of ways to control their obsessions, they are less effective in their efforts to control their thoughts than people without OCD. In addition, individuals with OCD tend to rely more often on ineffective control strategies, like compulsions, self-criticism, and avoidance. Efforts to control the obsession are exhausting and make it difficult to focus on other tasks at hand. The effort is seldom worth the payoff.

FOCUS EXERCISE 2.5:
WHAT CONTROL STRATEGIES DO YOU USE?

In your notebook, use a scale of 0 to 4 to rate how often you use each of these control strategies to deal with your obsession.

Control Strategy	Not at all	Some-times	Often	Very Often	Most of the Time
1. Avoidance	0	1	2	3	4
2. Trying to convince yourself	0	1	2	3	4
3. Thought-stopping	0	1	2	3	4
4. Self-criticism	0	1	2	3	4
5. Distraction	0	1	2	3	4
6. Thought replacement	0	1	2	3	4

If your responses were mostly 3s and 4s, it means that you are trying very hard to control your thoughts, which may be making your obsessions worse. You will want to revisit this issue in later chapters when you begin treating the problem.

CHAPTER 3

The Making of an Obsession

WHY DO YOU HAVE OBSESSIONS AND COMPULSIONS?

At this time, no one knows for sure why OCD develops. We are starting to get a reasonable understanding of why it may persist, however. This is good news, because in knowing why OCD persists, there is a road map for determining how to overcome it.

ENGAGING OBSESSIONAL THOUGHTS

You may recall from chapter 2 that the average person has approximately 4,000 distinct thoughts per day, and that many of these thoughts appear quite spontaneously with little or no connection to a current task. Furthermore, most people have "normal obsessions." If it is true that most people have unwanted intrusive thoughts, and everyone has hundreds of spontaneous thoughts in a typical day, why do some people have such a problem with two or three different types of thoughts?

The answer lies in how you respond to the thought: do you feel the need to engage the thought, or are you able to dismiss it as unimportant? Engaging the thought means taking it very seriously and assuming that it signals the potential for harm, threat, or danger, so that it becomes ever more meaningful and important. Take the following example. Larry was a salesperson who had to fly frequently. Every time Larry was about to pass through airport security, he would get the sudden impulse to blurt out the word "bomb." Of course, actually doing so would have serious consequences, especially with heightened security sensitivities following 9/11. Larry became extremely anxious about having to fly anywhere. Eventually he was unable to get the word "bomb" out of his head, no matter what he did, and finally he declined to fly altogether.

What makes Larry so anxious about this impulse to blurt out the word "bomb"? Larry becomes anxious because he engages the thought. When he has the thought, he begins to wonder whether having the thought is going to cause him to actually lose control and blurt it out. He wonders if the fact that he has this impulse means that maybe he has a hidden self-destructive side that he has never realized before. He assumes that the fact that he cannot control the thought means that it must be very important and meaningful; either that it is a prophetic warning sign that he is going to actually blurt out the word "bomb," or that he is losing mental control and, therefore, behavioral control. He is also devastated by the idea that he might end up putting the security personnel through such trouble; as a conscientious, law-abiding person, the idea of triggering a false alarm is distressing to him. By the time he sought help, Larry was convinced he was quite capable of losing control and acting on the thought. It would be hard for Larry to interpret the thought this way and *not* feel very anxious about it.

THINKING ABOUT THOUGHTS

Thoughts enter and exit conscious awareness at breakneck speed. All of us are constantly evaluating what we see, whether we like it or dislike it, find it beautiful or ugly, think it is good or bad, or think it is threatening or safe. We evaluate our internal experiences, as well. For example, we try to determine whether an ache, pain, or other bodily sensation might indicate a serious illness (such as a heart attack) or whether it is just an upset stomach. Likewise, we constantly evaluate our thoughts, ideas, and memories with other thoughts, such as "That's a pleasant thought," "What a stupid idea," "That's an interesting idea," "What an upsetting thought," "What a funny thought." This is where the earlier idea of "engaging with thoughts" comes from. Hundreds of times during the day, we make automatic judgments as to whether our thoughts are good or bad, meaningful or meaningless, threatening or nonthreatening. The more meaningful and important a thought, the more likely we are to engage the thought.

FOCUS EXERCISE 3.1: PERCEIVED IMPORTANCE OF THOUGHTS

In your notebook, draw two columns. Label the left column "unwanted intrusive thoughts I consider important" and label the right column "unwanted intrusive thoughts I consider unimportant." Try to think of five to ten examples to put in each column. For the important intrusive thoughts, you can refer back to Focus Exercise 2.2, as the thoughts you identified as obsessions are likely to be important (even if part of you knows your obsession is unimportant). You might find it more difficult to identify unimportant intrusive thoughts because they tend to be forgotten very quickly. If you can't come up with examples of unimportant intrusive thoughts right now, monitor your thoughts over the next hour and then do the exercise.

Once you have identified five to ten important and unimportant intrusive thoughts, go back and write down what makes these thoughts important to you or unimportant to you. The following is an example of what Eliska wrote down for her important and unimportant intrusive thoughts.

Important Intrusive Thoughts	Unimportant Intrusive Thoughts
Impulse to swear during a religious ceremony	Impulse to pull a fire alarm
"Have I committed an unforgivable sin against God?"	"Did I sign that check?"
"Did I contaminate my religious observance by having an impure thought?"	"Was that surface dirty?"

Note that these are examples relevant to Eliska. Even though you might consider the thoughts in the right-hand column highly important, she does not, because she is not threatened by them. What made the first thought in the left-hand column so threatening to her is that she believed that having thoughts about blasphemous acts was as sinful, morally, as actually doing those acts. The second and third thoughts were threatening because she believed that the nagging sense of doubt she experienced meant that it was likely she had committed an unforgivable sin or contaminated a prayer, and needed to atone (in the first instance) and repeat the prayer (in the second instance). To Eliska, ignoring this sense of doubt was the same thing as deliberately sinning. The appearance of these thoughts also suggested to her that maybe at heart she is not a true believer in God, a devastating idea to her. The first thought in the right-hand column caused her no distress because she was fully confident in her degree of self-control. The second thought caused her no distress because she was confident in her memory and competence. The third thought didn't bother her because she believed that she had a strong immune system that would readily withstand contact with germs. This is noteworthy because fears of contamination, of doing something socially inappropriate (such as pulling a fire alarm), and of making a mistake are common obsessions that are highly impairing for some people with OCD.

Eliska's appraisals of the thoughts in the left-hand column are based on erroneous information about thoughts and thought processes (e.g., that thoughts cause action or that thoughts must reflect personality). Her ideas about personal responsibility are also overvalued or extreme (that having the very idea that you have been responsible for a negative event is identical to deliberately causing the negative event). We refer to this as "incorrect appraisal," or "faulty appraisal."

THE COGNITIVE BEHAVIORAL MODEL

In the last decade psychologists have gained new understanding on why obsessions and compulsions become so frequent and distressing. Chapter 1 introduced cognitive behavioral therapy, which is the term used for a new model and treatment of OCD that developed from the work of Dr. S. Rachman (1997) and Salkovskis (1996). The CBT model proposes that obsessions and compulsions persist because of individuals' faulty or erroneous ways of evaluating their unwanted intrusive thoughts, as well as their attempts to control them. In other words, obsessional thoughts become a problem when they give rise to faulty appraisals (cognition) and ineffective attempts to control the thought and the distress it causes.

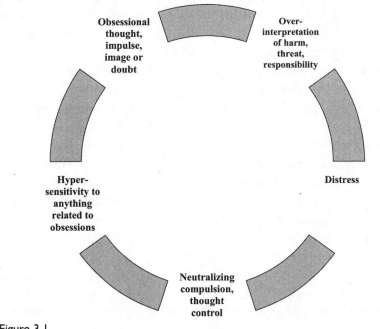

Figure 3.1

As can be seen from Figure 3.1, the cognitive behavioral approach suggests that an obsession develops and persists because the obsession is overinterpreted as signifying harm, danger, or threat, and as making you responsible for potentially causing harm. It is difficult to have such concerns and feel calm and relaxed; when the thought is interpreted in this manner, you become distressed. You then seek to reduce this distress by performing a compulsion, neutralization, avoidance, or mental control strategy. All of the strategies used to manage the distress associated with the thought actually become triggers for the thought, and so thought frequency escalates. Your mind becomes extremely efficient at detecting anything related to the obsession. As Salkovskis (personal communication) has suggested, women who have recently become pregnant suddenly begin to notice pregnant women, babies, strollers, and so on because these things are suddenly very relevant to their condition. Let's discuss the central components in detail.

Obsessional Thoughts

The CBT model of OCD begins with the assertion that everyone has unwanted intrusive thoughts. It is likely that thoughts, images, or impulses that are relevant to your most important goals and sense of identity are the ones most likely to grab your attention. For example, a woman who prides herself on her gentle nature and consideration to others may be especially taken aback by the sudden impulse to spit on a friend who is talking to her, whereas a person who does not value being considerate may not be particularly phased by such a thought. Salkovskis (1985) argued that obsessions derive from current concerns. Recent research testing this hypothesis supports the idea; intrusive thoughts that become obsessions tend to be thoughts that reflect current concerns or issues (Rowa, Purdon, Summerfeldt, and Antony, forthcoming) and tend to be inconsistent with the attributes you value the most. For example, Ayisha had thoughts of pushing others in front of the subway train. She reported that she had experienced those thoughts for several years and was able to readily dismiss them, but that after she began considering a career in a helping profession, these same thoughts became very upsetting; she started to wonder if these thoughts were revealing a highly violent, antisocial side to her personality that would make her extremely dangerous were she to work in a helping profession.

Overinterpretation of the Meaning of the Thought

Once an unwanted intrusive thought gets your attention, you will automatically engage in some appraisal or evaluation of the thought. Rachman (1997) contends that people with OCD engage in a catastrophic misinterpretation of their intrusive thoughts' significance. An example of a catastrophic misinterpretation would be when a man has a thought of exposing himself in public and then interprets the occurrence of this thought to mean he is in danger of doing it because he believes "thoughts can lead to actions." In another example, a woman has a repulsive image of dropping her baby and concludes she is unsafe around the baby because she harbors latent (unconscious) resentment toward the child. In the past few years, psychologists have identified a number of different types of faulty appraisals that are involved in the persistence of obsessional thinking. Together, these faulty appraisals lead to the erroneous conclusion that the obsession is a highly significant symptom that could lead to dire consequences for yourself or for others, unless some action is taken to control it. Here is a brief overview of the faulty appraisals that can turn intrusive thoughts into obsessions:

Inflated Responsibility

This construct was introduced by Salkovskis (1996) and refers to the belief that if you have any influence over a negative outcome whatsoever, then you are responsible for doing whatever you can to prevent that outcome, and indeed are honor bound to do so, no matter how minute the probability of that negative outcome is. For example, Kuan-Yin noticed that when the wind blew in a certain direction, the branches of a tree on the corner near his house occasionally interfered with a clear view of a stop sign. He called the city and reported the problem, but no action was taken and shortly thereafter an accident happened at the intersection. Kuan-Yin felt responsible for the accident because he thinks he should have done more to convince the city to trim the tree or should have trimmed it himself. He felt that his inaction was criminally negligent, as bad as if he had actually taken the stop sign away.

Susan was studying at the library and decided to eat her peanut butter cookie. About an hour after she left the library, Susan suddenly thought, "What if there are crumbs from my cookie on the cubicle and what if the next person who sits there has a peanut allergy? The person wouldn't expect there to be any food substances there. What if he or she touches my crumbs and has a full-blown anaphylactic reaction, and doesn't have his or her medicine and dies? It would be entirely my fault!" Susan feels as guilty and distressed over her "carelessness" in leaving cookie crumbs behind as if she had directly attempted to murder someone.

Overestimation of Threat

This refers to a tendency to overestimate the severity and/or the likelihood of imagined negative consequences of an obsession. When Delia prayed in church, a terrible profanity would pop into her mind. She assumed this was a sign of demon possession, and that if she did not stop having this thought, she would be eternally damned, a horrific idea to someone of her faith. Gustav, a lawyer, was plagued with sudden impulses to say something extremely inappropriate in court. Even though he had no history of impulsive behavior of any kind, and was actually known for being very calm and controlled in the courtroom, he estimated the probability of his acting on these impulses as 65 percent.

Thought-Action Fusion

This is the assumption that thinking about a negative event increases its likelihood of actually happening, and/or that "bad" thoughts are morally equivalent to "bad" deeds (Rachman and Shafran 1999). In the week prior to the space shuttle launch in the fall of 1985, Reina, who was an avid follower of the space program, had a sudden image of the shuttle exploding. She was horrified and did her best to keep it out of her head, believing that thinking about it would cause it to happen. She avoided all news stories on the shuttle and stopped watching TV and reading the paper altogether during that week. When the terrible disaster happened, Reina believed that her thoughts had caused it to happen and was still guilt ridden almost two decades later. Xuan has images of engaging in a sexual act with a woman who is not his wife and to whom he is not at all attracted. Xuan believes that having this thought is as bad as actually cheating on his wife—that he has been unfaithful, and is therefore an immoral person.

Mental Control

This refers to the belief that it is necessary to exert control over unwanted thoughts in order to maintain mental health and good behavioral control. Fahad was a traveling sales representative who had frequent intrusive images of driving his car into oncoming traffic. He believed that it was very dangerous to allow himself to have these thoughts, fearing that loss of control over the thought might lead to a loss of control over his behavior. Kathy had repugnant thoughts of molesting her child. She was convinced that she had to stop these thoughts from entering her mind for fear that eventually she might act on them.

Intolerance of Uncertainty

This refers to the belief that you need perfect certainty that something bad has not or will not happen before you can make a decision or continue with your daily activities. Anke lived in constant doubt as to whether or not she had committed an unpardonable sin. She repeatedly reviewed all her daily actions in a desperate attempt to determine for certain whether anything she had done might be sinful. Jane had intrusive thoughts that maybe she was sexually aroused by violence and therefore might be capable of rape. She spent hours reading about rapists and matching known qualities of rapists with her own qualities. Indeed, she thought that learning that she was, in fact, a potential rapist would be a relief to the feeling of uncertainty. At least then she could withdraw from society and forgo having friends and a family of her own, knowing with full confidence that she was doing the right thing.

Perfectionism

This is the belief that there is one correct solution to every problem and that anything less than perfect is wholly inadequate. Eliska believed that an entire religious observance was contaminated if she had even a fleeting trace of an "impure" thought while conducting it.

Failures in Thought Control

Many people with OCD have erroneous beliefs about the meaning of failures in thought control. These include the fear that if they don't try to control the thought it will escalate continuously until they "go crazy" or "break down." Failures in thought control are also interpreted as evidence that the thought must be meaningful; why else would it keep recurring despite your best efforts? Finally, people may assume that failures in mental control will lead to failures in control over their behavior.

Compulsions, Neutralization, and Thought Control

It would be hard to imagine someone appraising his or her intrusive thoughts in one or more of the ways described above and not perceiving them as a threat. When people feel threatened, they become distressed and focused on coping with the threat, by engaging in some sort of action that reduces the sense of threat. Such actions could involve a compulsion, like checking or seeking reassurance from others, neutralization, like trying to rationalize that you are not a sinner or a bad parent, for example, and suppression of the unwanted thought (see chapter 2 for a review of compulsions, neutralization, and mental control strategies).

Short-Term Gain for Long-Term Pain

Most people with OCD feel some relief after engaging in some compulsion or neutralizing behavior, either because their negative feelings have decreased or because they feel as if they have staved off even worse distress. At first glance, this strategy would seem to work, but herein lies the problem: the strategy does not allow you to learn about the true threat represented by the obsession. Instead, the reduction in distress the strategy affords makes it increasingly harder to resist doing the same thing in response to the obsession the next time. Efforts to control the thought make sense in the moment but again lead to long-term problems: control efforts sometimes fail and require considerable effort, so they are exhausting.

Increased Frequency of Obsessions

When you use neutralizing acts and compulsions, they come to remind you of the obsession, because they are so closely linked with it. For example, Juan had obsessions of stabbing his grandchildren and would neutralize these thoughts by constructing a vivid mental picture of his grandchildren as healthy, successful adults. In one image, they would be all wearing graduation robes. Whenever Juan saw an article of clothing similar to those that his grandchildren were wearing in his "good" thought, the obsession would immediately come to mind. Unfortunately, when you try to suppress a thought, you actually become extremely sensitive to anything related to the thought, so the thought is easily triggered. Thus, compulsions, neutralizing, and thought control make you overly attend to anything related to the obsession, which in turn triggers the obsession. Hence you experience an increase in the frequency of the obsession.

A TREATMENT RATIONALE

The cognitive behavioral model of obsessions provides many clues into how you can defeat the vicious cycle of obsessional thinking. According to the model, obsessions become more frequent and upsetting when they give rise to faulty appraisals and when you use compulsions and other neutralization strategies to manage the obsession and reduce the distress it causes.

Chapters 8 through 10 provide detailed information and cognitive behavioral strategies that you can use to break the vicious cycle of obsessions. The goal of these interventions is to help you move an obsession from the category of an *important intrusive thought* to the category of an *unimportant thought*. More specifically, cognitive behavioral interventions are aimed at the following:

- replacing faulty appraisals of an obsession with a balanced view of the meaning of an obsession

- preventing or eliminating compulsions and other neutralizing strategies

- learning that obsessions, no matter how disgusting or bizarre, can be left alone without any negative consequence

CHAPTER 4

Establishing Your Symptom Profile

YOUR OWN OCD SYMPTOMS

The previous chapters have reviewed what OCD is and presented you with the reasons why OCD persists. Now it is time for you to establish a clear understanding of your own OCD symptoms. You should to plan to spend two weeks on this chapter. You may be thinking, "I already know what my OCD is like. I know what symptoms I have!" What we have found in our clinical work is that compulsions, neutralizing, thought control, and avoidance can become so second nature to people that they often don't realize they are doing them or don't realize that what they are doing is actually part of their OCD. For example, Juan had violent images of harming his grandchildren. In order to avoid having these horrendous thoughts, he avoided anything that triggered them, including the color red, which reminded him of blood. However, this had been happening for so long that he was used to not wearing red clothes, not driving his son's red car, not eating in restaurants that had red booths, and so forth. He no longer even recognized this as part of his OCD, but rather saw it as part of a color preference. Furthermore, most people are unaware of the kinds of appraisals they make about the meaning of their obsessions; these appraisals tend to happen automatically and it requires considerable practice to be able to identify them.

In order for you to be able to overcome your OCD, it is crucial that you have a comprehensive understanding of all of your obsessions, compulsions, neutralizing, thought control, and avoidance (that is, the behavioral part of your OCD), as well as the different ways you interpret the meaning of having your obsessions (that is, the cognitive part of your OCD). The exercises in this chapter will help you establish a better understanding. Let's begin with the behavioral part of your OCD.

ESTABLISHING YOUR SYMPTOM PROFILE: THE BEHAVIORAL COMPONENT

For the next week, monitor the occurrence of your obsessions and your use of compulsions, neutralizing, thought control, and avoidance. To help you with this, we will provide some definitions of each: Compulsions and neutralizing are any mental or physical actions you engage in to reduce the distress you feel as a result of your obsession. Thought control is any deliberate attempt to get rid of a thought once it occurs. Avoidance is any action, person, place, situation, or object that you steer clear of as you try to prevent yourself from having the obsession or reduce your distress if the obsession occurs. (Refer to chapter 2 if you need further assistance in identifying your obsessions, compulsions, neutralizing, thought control, and avoidance.)

Compulsions and neutralizing are any mental or physical actions you engage in to reduce the distress you feel as a result of your obsession.

FOCUS EXERCISE 4.1:
MONITORING OCD BEHAVIORS

In your notebook, make six columns. Label them, from left to right, as follows:

- date

- obsession

- feelings (e.g., disgust, fear)

- compulsions/neutralizing

- thought control

- feelings after use of compulsions/neutralizing

For the next week, monitor your obsessions. When an obsession occurs, write the date and what the obsession was. In the feelings column, write all of the feelings you had when the obsession happened. Rate how intense those feelings were. Use a 0 to 100 rating scale where 0 equals no emotion, 50 equals moderately intense emotion, and 100 equals the most intense emotion you have ever experienced. Next, record all of the compulsions and/or neutralizing strategies you used in response to the obsession, as well as any thought-control strategies you used to try to get rid of the obsession. Finally, rate the level of emotion you felt after you completed each compulsion/neutralizing strategy (how much you felt relieved, less anxious, etc.).

Because obsessions can occur so frequently, we recommend that you report on only three occurrences of the obsession per day: one in the morning of each day, one in the afternoon of each day, and one in the evening of each day. If you do this for seven days, this will make a total of twenty-one entries. It is important that you complete the form as soon as possible after the episode you are reporting on. You may want to keep your notebook with you at all times.

The following is a day from a chart completed by Richard, whose primary obsession is that he might be a pedophile.

Date	Obsession	Feelings	Compulsions/ Neutralizing	Thought Control	Feelings Afterwards
Jan. 21- morn.	"Did I find it arousing to see those girls playing?"	Shame-100 Fear-90 Guilt-90	Pictured the girls as healthy, happy adults	None	Shame-50 Fear-80 Guilt-90
Jan. 21- aft.	"What if I am a pedophile?"	Shame-80 Fear-80	Went back on that Internet Web site to see how much I am like known pedophiles	Tried to suppress the thought, but couldn't	Shame-30 Fear-70
Jan. 21- even.	"Did I linger on that children's TV station when I was changing channels?"	Fear-40 Guilt-20 Shame-20	None. Thought suppression worked.	Distracted myself from the thought by focusing on the football game	Fear-5 Guilt-5 Shame-10

Now, during this same week, keep track of all of the avoidance you engage in. Use separate pages in your notebook and simply keep a log. Each time you avoid someone, something, or some situation, write down the date and what you were avoiding. Keep track of both total avoidance (declining to visit your grandchildren altogether) and avoidance of certain features of a situation (agreeing to visit your grandchildren but avoiding being alone with them in a room).

ESTABLISHING YOUR SYMPTOM PROFILE: THE COGNITIVE COMPONENT

Chapter 3 presented an overview of the ways people with repugnant obsessions tend to interpret the meaning of those obsessions. Now it is time for you to identify all the different ways you interpret your obsessions. This is a bit harder and requires practice because, as mentioned earlier, these interpretations happen automatically, leaving you with impressions about the obsessions before you are even aware that these impressions are based on a series of assumptions. The human mind is actually geared to work very efficiently, and people often take mental shortcuts. For example, when you see a table, you see a table; however, somewhere in the back of your mind, your brain has processed the visual data it has received about this series of inclined planes and has generated the conclusion that it is a table, without you even knowing that that level of processing has taken place.

Here's another example. Deborah gets out of her limousine and begins walking briskly down the street. She is wearing her fur coat and her designer sunglasses and sports a large diamond ring on her finger and a Rolex watch. She is in a hurry because she is late for her appointment with a manicurist and her driver couldn't let her off right in front of the door. A panhandler is sitting on the street just near the entrance to the beauty spa where she is headed. Answer the following question with a yes/no answer *immediately:* Will she give him any money, yes or no? What was your *immediate,* honest answer? Now, think about what led you to generate an answer. Chances are, you answered yes or no based on an automatic processing of the information you were given. Your answer probably depended upon your views of what wealthy people are like, what people who wear fur coats are like, and/or what women are like.

Now that you've had time to consider the situation, you may change your answer. For example, you may now consider that the fact that Deborah was rushing to the appointment means that she has demonstrated some consideration for others' time, and so she may be empathic and considerate enough to give money to someone. Or, you may decide that she is in a hurry only because she has somewhere else to go after the manicure, and conclude that she is a self-absorbed and self-interested person. Or, you may conclude that you simply don't have enough information to answer either way, and you may want more information (for example, you may want to know if Deborah has a history of giving money to panhandlers or if she is liberal or conservative in her views toward homeless people). That's the beauty of revisiting automatic impressions of events, including your own thoughts! It's what you might call the "sober second thought" about situations, where you can take the time to consider all the angles, seek new information about a situation, and draw a conclusion based on all the available data, rather than taking your first opinion for granted.

We want you to begin understanding your automatic appraisals of your obsessions just as you examined your original appraisal of Deborah.

For each obsession you experience, ask yourself questions like these:

- "What does this obsession mean about my personality?"

- "What does this obsession mean for the future?"

- "What is it that bothers me the most about having this obsession?"

For example, Paula experienced obsessions about molesting her child. She asked herself, "What bothers me so much about this obsession?" Her answer was, "Good mothers do not have thoughts of harming their babies, so the fact that I have the obsession means that I am not a good mother," and "I might lose control and act on it and harm my baby," and "I don't know why I would have a thought like this, unless there is a perverted part of me that I never knew about before." It is these appraisals that Paula needs to question. Note that Paula's desire to protect her child from molestation is wholly appropriate and rational; we would never want to make Paula develop a callous attitude toward her child or try to trivialize the consequences of her child being molested. Instead, we want Paula to question her view that having the obsession *itself* makes her a bad mother and that the obsession *itself* is the route by which harm might occur to her child.

Identifying Your Overinterpretations

Next, you will record your appraisal of your obsessions in your notebook. Repugnant obsessions typically concern themes and actions that anyone would rate as disgusting or, at the very least, unpleasant. You might find that at first you are just writing down "It's disgusting" or "I hate this obsession." These thoughts are accurate descriptions of the thoughts and your response to them; of course you find the obsession disgusting and hateful.

However, you won't find this information very helpful. What you need to do is figure out all the reasons why you hate the thought as much as you do, to the point where you realize that your response to it is so intense that it interferes with your life; that is, you will want to discover what it is that makes your reaction to the thought so intense. Keep in mind that many people experience thoughts that are equally repugnant, but they are not bothered by them because they interpret them as having no personal significance ("What an awful thought! Thank goodness I'm not the kind of person who would ever act on it!" or "What an awful, unusual thought. I guess one downside of my creative mind is that it generates unpleasant, as well as pleasant, thoughts").

FOCUS EXERCISE 4.2: MONITORING YOUR APPRAISAL

In your notebook, make four columns. The columns, from left to right, are as follows:

- date

- obsession

- feelings

- appraisal of the obsession

For the next week, monitor your obsessions. When an obsession occurs, write down the date and what the obsession was. In the feelings column, write all of the feelings you had when the obsession happened. Rate how intense those feelings were using the scale you used in the previous exercise. Next, record all of the thoughts you had about the obsession when it occurred.

Because obsessions can occur so frequently, we recommend that you report on only three occurrences of the obsession per day: one in the morning, one in the afternoon, and one in the evening. If you do this for seven days, you will have a total of twenty-one entries. It is important that you complete the form as soon as possible after the episode you are reporting on. You may want to keep your notebook with you at all times.

The following is a day from Daphne's chart.

Date	Obsession	Feelings	Appraisal
Jan. 28-morn.	Impulse to kick out the crutch of an injured person	Fear-90 Shame-80	Am I a psychopath?? I wouldn't be having thoughts like this unless part of me truly wanted to do it. The more I have these thoughts, the more likely I am to act on them! I am a menace to society. I am a bad person for having these thoughts.
Jan. 28-aft.	What if some water spilled on the floor from the drinking fountain and someone slipped and hurt themselves?	Fear-80 Guilt-90	I don't think any water spilled, but maybe it did, and if anything happened, it would be all my fault. Not going back to clean up any water is just like actually tripping someone.
Jan. 28-even.	Urge to trip elderly person	Fear-90 Guilt-90 Shame-90	I am a bad person. These thoughts keep happening even though I don't want them to! They must be a sign of something; maybe I want to do it; maybe I am a cold, callous person at heart, and this is a sign that I shouldn't go into nursing. I'm going to lose control and do it. Not controlling this thought is the same as actually tripping someone.

Note that the appraisals you record in the fourth column should explain all the feelings you recorded in the third column. That is, if you record fear in column three, the appraisals in the fourth column should explain why you are feeling that way. If you feel fear and shame and guilt, you might be reporting such appraisals as, "Oh my gosh, what if I lose control and act on the thought!" (which explains why you feel fearful) and "Good, moral people don't have thoughts like this; this thought means I am an immoral person!" (which explains shame, guilt).

Here are some questions that may help you identify your automatic appraisal of the obsession. You may want to copy these directly into your notebook to use as a guide:

- "What does this obsession mean about my personality?"

- "What kind of person would I be if I didn't do anything about this obsession?"

- "What does it mean that the obsession keeps coming back?"

- "What might happen if I didn't do anything about this obsession?"

At the end of these seven days, your reactions to your obsessions should make a lot more sense to you. You should have a better understanding of why your obsessions cause so many emotions and why you behave the way you do in response to them. There is little doubt that there is good internal logic to your OCD; that is, your interpretation of the meaning of an obsession explains your emotional response and the coping strategies you use to manage that response. You may also have noticed that you were making assumptions without having thought them through to their logical conclusion.

CHAPTER 5

Why Does Your OCD Persist?

WHY DOES YOUR OCD PERSIST?

Now that you've spent two weeks monitoring your OCD symptoms, let's make sure that you have a solid understanding of why they persist, even though you don't want to have them. Understanding why your symptoms persist will help you understand the rationale behind our suggestions for overcoming them.

BEHAVIORAL FACTORS

Review your monitoring forms in Focus Exercise 4.1. Specifically, look at how you felt before you engaged in your compulsions, neutralizing, and avoidance, or how you might have felt if you hadn't completed them. Chances are you are doing these acts because they make you feel better in some way, or because you believe you would feel even worse if you didn't do them. So the compulsions, neutralizing, and avoidance behaviors serve the purpose of reducing discomfort in the short term. Any behavior that reduces an unpleasant feeling is one that people will repeat; this is a fundamental human truth. You keep repeating these actions because they make you feel better, or at the very least they make you feel as if you are preventing worse discomfort.

Even if you want to stop, the quest for relief from the discomfort associated with the obsession will compel you to continue.

The more often you do these behaviors, the more normal they become to you and the more likely they are to become a habit. You may be doing them without even consciously seeking relief. Habits are hard to break; think about some other habits you might have that you have vowed many times to break, such as nail-biting, snacking on junk food, watching too much TV, or spending rather than saving. Even if you think your OCD behaviors are excessive, absurd, or ridiculous, you do them because they have worked in the past to reduce discomfort, or they have become habitual and therefore hard to resist. You are not crazy for doing them!

FOCUS EXERCISE 5.1: UNDERSTANDING THE PERSISTENCE OF OCD BEHAVIORS

Review your monitoring forms from Focus Exercise 4.1. Look at your emotions before and after the compulsions and neutralizing. Sometimes graphs can be really helpful in understanding how things work together. In your notebook, make a graph like this one:

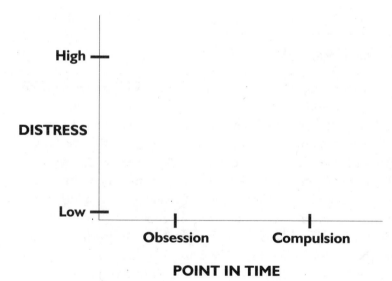

Now, make a dot on the graph that best reflects your discomfort level prior to having the obsession. For example, if you experienced moderate distress, your dot would be about halfway up the "distress" line, to the left of the point reading "obsession." Now make a dot that reflects your discomfort level immediately after getting the obsession. Now make a dot that reflects your discomfort level after completing the compulsion. Now join the dots. If your discomfort increased after performing the compulsion/neutralizing act, plot what you expect your discomfort would have been if you had done nothing in response to the obsession at that time. Chances are, your discomfort shot up when you had the obsession and reduced considerably when you performed the compulsion or neutralizing act.

PUTTING IT ALL TOGETHER

Obsessions and compulsions occur in cyclical fashion. As an obsession occurs, you interpret it as signaling harm or danger, or immorality. This interpretation results in great discomfort. The compulsion or neutralizing act reduces that discomfort (or at least keeps it lower than what you would expect if you refrained from performing it). In terminating exposure to the obsession, you learn no new information about the obsession, and so your original interpretation that the obsession is dangerous or threatening survives intact. Meanwhile, attempts to avoid having the obsession make you hypersensitive to anything related to the obsession (which includes anything to do with your compulsions, neutralizing, and avoidance), which in turn makes the obsession more likely to occur, and the whole cycle starts again.

FOCUS EXERCISE 5.2: MASTERING YOUR UNDERSTANDING OF THE OCD CYCLE

Before leaving this chapter, try one more exercise to help you see how the cognitive behavioral model looks at the persistence of obsessions. Pick one of the "unimportant" intrusive thoughts that you recorded in the right-hand column in Focus Exercise 3.1. Now imagine how you might have to think in order to change this thought from an unimportant intrusion into a really upsetting obsessional thought. Record in your notebook what would make these intrusions bother you to the same degree that your obsessional thoughts do. Think about how you might need to exaggerate your personal sense of responsibility over the thought, its perceived threat, or the importance of controlling the thought. What types of efforts to control the thought do you think would make it worse? What kinds of consequences could you imagine if you failed to control the thought? After you have created a hypothetical vicious cycle, can you see how someone might actually develop an obsession from such a thought?

If you have done this as advised, you should now have a much better understanding of your obsessions and compulsions. So where do you go from here? First, you will start by dealing with your interpretations of the obsessions as guesses, rather than truths or facts. We are also going to give you lots of information about thoughts and thought processes that will help you learn to regard your evaluations (appraisals) of the obsession as guesses and not facts. Finally, we are going to help you start the process of changing how you deal with your obsession, moving you from using control, avoidance, and compulsions/neutralizing to tolerating the obsession without doing anything in response to it. So, armed with this new cognitive behavioral understanding of obsessions, it's time to begin the process of reclaiming your life from OCD.

CHAPTER 6

Are You Ready to Make Changes?

CHANGE CAN BE DIFFICULT

Obsessions can be repulsive and the strategies you use to manage them, such as compulsions, neutralizing, avoidance, or thought control, are time-consuming, frustrating, and not reliably effective. Yet, these strategies have no doubt rescued you from distress, at least at times. Outside the obsession-compulsion cycle, you may recognize your obsessions as improbable or ridiculous, and the strategies you use to manage them as excessive, overly precautious, or silly. Inside the obsession-compulsion cycle, the strategies feel necessary. It is not unusual to feel two ways about the strategies you use to manage your obsessions. It is also not unusual to feel conflicted about making changes in how you manage obsessions. Sometimes people find it hard to give up their coping strategies, even when they know it may afford them some relief from OCD. The purpose of this chapter is to help you identify and overcome obstacles to overcoming your OCD.

CONCEALMENT OF OBSESSIONS

The first problem that can interfere with treatment is concealment. You may well be inclined to keep these kinds of thoughts to yourself, worrying about how others might react. However, in order to tackle your problem with them, it may be important for you to reveal your obsessions to at least one or two people. Some of the exercises this book recommends require that you seek normative information from others, such as friends and spiritual advisors, about obsessional thoughts. Some religious obsessions (such as "God is evil") may be so disturbing that verbalizing the thought to another person seems sinful. If you have never disclosed your problem with obsessions to anyone, you will have difficulty making use of our treatment recommendations. You need to believe that it's okay to have these thoughts or doubts. As long as you conceal the obsession, it is difficult to seek important information about the thought and give yourself the permission you need to have the thought.

Although some of these exercises require that you share the content of some of your obsessions with others, be advised that we want you to choose people who are likely to be sympathetic and/or who have some knowledge and experience with OCD. For example, some spiritual advisors have more experience with and better knowledge of OCD than others. Furthermore, it is not necessary to disclose the existence of your obsessions to everyone with whom you come in contact. Instead, choose appropriate and suitable people.

OVERVALUED IDEATION

A second obstacle to successful treatment is overvalued ideation. This refers to your belief in your interpretation of an obsession ("There is absolutely no way a person can have a thought about a violent/sinful/sexual act unless they truly are a violent/sinful/perverse person at heart"). If you truly believe that having an intrusive thought, such as "Was I sexually aroused by a same sex person?" constitutes a sin against God that He will punish, then it will be quite difficult to allow yourself to purposefully think the thought. If this is the case for you, we recommend that you consult your spiritual advisor to determine whether there are circumstances under which it is not a sin to deliberately think such thoughts, such as for the purpose of overcoming an obsessional problem. The following exercise may also help you.

FOCUS EXERCISE 6.1: OVERCOMING OVERVALUED IDEATION

For this exercise, make a table with two columns, the left-hand one labeled "original appraisal" and the right-hand one labeled "appraisal expressed in the conditional." Now turn back to Focus Exercise 4.2, in which you recorded your appraisal of your obsessional thoughts. In the left-hand column, write the most important appraisal of your obsessional thoughts; that is, record the appraisal that is associated with the most distress. In the right-hand column, reword the appraisal in a way that qualifies it, or makes it conditional. Here are some examples:

Original Appraisal	Appraisal Expressed in the Conditional
"I am a cold, callous person for having this thought."	"I might be a cold, callous person for having this thought."
"I must be a pedophile for having this thought."	"I might be a pedophile for having this thought."
"Having a sinful thought means I am condemned to Hell."	"Having a sinful thought might mean that I am condemned to Hell."

Now that you have done this, look at the appraisals in the right-hand column. Notice how, in rephrasing the appraisal, your mind can open itself to competing ideas about the thought. In treating the appraisal as a guess rather than as a truth, you can become receptive to reasons for or circumstances under which your appraisal might not be valid. Again, consult your spiritual advisor for guidance with this latter exercise if you find it difficult to do on your own.

CONCERNS ABOUT OVERCOMING OCD

Even if concealment and overvalued ideation are not issues for you, you may still have concerns about overcoming OCD. The fact that you are reading this book suggests that you are, at the very least, thinking about taking steps to overcoming your OCD. Thus, you are clearly motivated at some level to get rid of your OCD. We do recognize, though, that you may feel that treatment of your OCD could actually cost you. In a recent study examining fears that people with OCD have about treatment (Purdon, Rowa, and Antony 2004), participants expressed such concerns as these:

- "The treatment will not be effective and I will be a hopeless case."

- "If I get better, others will have expectations of me that I do not feel I could meet."

- "I'm concerned about reliving past experiences I've put out of my mind."

- "I fear that treatment will make my symptoms worse."

- "I fear that if I change, my husband and family will not like the new me."

Some fears may not be that straightforward. You may be concerned that if you do get better, your family will be angry with you for not doing it sooner ("If he could do it now, why couldn't he do it two years ago?"). You may also anticipate losing face when you no longer need to do rituals that you currently abide by and have vehemently enforced, despite inconvenience to others. Overcoming OCD means acknowledging to yourself and to others that compulsions, neutralizing, and avoidance are unnecessary. You may fear that if you overcome your OCD, you will no longer receive the same degree of emotional support and attention from your family. You may fear the unknown and so would rather keep your OCD, regardless of suffering, because of concern that change could be worse.

FOCUS EXERCISE 6.2: IDENTIFYING YOUR CONCERNS ABOUT OVERCOMING OCD

In your notebook, list all the concerns or fears you have about the idea of overcoming your OCD. Remember, it's okay to feel conflicted about getting better. It is much better to acknowledge your concerns and address them than to ignore them.

ADDRESSING SPECIFIC FEARS AND CONCERNS ABOUT OVERCOMING OCD

As with many fears, your fears of overcoming OCD may not be as well-grounded as they feel. When people are afraid of something, they often don't think the fear through to its logical conclusion. For example, Dan was afraid of spiders because he believed that they would lay eggs in his ears. When he talked through this fear and considered that the spiders common to his geographic region actually lay their eggs in their web, and that his ears were not the kind of place where spiders spin their webs, he was considerably less afraid of spiders. This next section helps you think about how realistic your fears actually are, once you have actually had a chance to think them through.

Fears About Others' Reactions

It is possible that if your OCD goes away, your family could have thoughts like, "Well, if it were that easy, why didn't she just get over it before?" or "He has been stringing us along!" and feel angry about having accommodated your compulsions, neutralizing, and avoidance strategies. But consider whether this would likely define your family's reaction to you for the rest of your life. First, people who love you and care about you will be happy to see you get your life back and will also be happy to get their lives back. Even if they have some anger about the past, this is likely to dissipate as they begin to enjoy your newfound flexibility, spontaneity, and freedom from fear. If not, there may be other, more serious problems in the relationship that exist independently of the OCD. If this is the case, you will be in a better position to cope if you don't have the stress of OCD on top of these other problems.

Another concern is that people will have much higher expectations of you if you recover from OCD. It is true that others' expectations of you may change if you do recover from your OCD. For example, your recovery could lead to a return to work or study, or a return to other obligations such as child care, household, and social responsibilities. It is important to recognize, though, that if you are free enough of your OCD to resume these responsibilities, you will be feeling substantially more confident, rested, relaxed, competent, and able to concentrate. Also keep in mind that your recovery from OCD will be gradual, and it is likely that as you recover, you will *naturally* begin to take on more and more responsibilities and activities. Thus, by the time you are fully recovered, you may well be functioning at full capacity in your various roles, and the expectations of others will be wholly in line with your abilities! You will want to, indeed, challenge yourself as you recover, so you can make the most of your new potential. The people around you are likely to be satisfied as long as you are trying to do your best.

Fears About the Treatment Itself

You have an excellent chance of overcoming your OCD as long as you follow the suggestions offered in this book—that is, as long as you actually do the exercises and apply them in your daily life, making time for them and accepting the challenges of treatment. If you do not benefit from this book, it may be that this is not a good time in your life to be trying to overcome your OCD, or you may need more intensive work with a therapist. Many people we have treated dread that they are going to be one of the minority who cannot benefit from treatment, but they are pleasantly surprised when they find themselves increasingly free of OCD. You will never know if you can benefit from treatment until you try. If you give this book a really good try, and it simply doesn't work for you, then you can pursue other treatment options, such as therapy with a qualified, knowledgeable therapist. It's better to try the treatment and either benefit from it (the most probable scenario) or learn that this approach doesn't work for you (and know to try something else) than it is to do nothing at all.

The treatment itself is scary because it requires you to take risks that are so averse to you that you have organized your life around avoiding them. However, these risks are acceptable, and no greater than risks that healthy, happy, successful people take many times on a daily basis. Furthermore, by the time you are asked to take certain risks, you will be ready for them. Don't judge your ability to take risks on your feelings about them right now.

Finally, it's important to understand that treatment cannot make your OCD worse. It is true that your distress and urge to use your coping strategies will heighten while you are doing the exposure exercises, but your overall distress between the exercises will decrease. We think of exposure exercises as short-term pain for long-term gain. If you were to sum up all the distress experienced during exposure, it would not come close to the amount of distress you would experience in a future of unrelenting OCD.

COSTS OF OCD: DO THEY OUTWEIGH YOUR CONCERNS?

Now that you have reviewed the concerns you may have about overcoming OCD and possibly reduced them, you can measure them against the costs of your OCD. You need to see whether the costs of your OCD outweigh the potential costs of overcoming OCD.

FOCUS EXERCISE 6.3: WHAT DOES YOUR OCD COST YOU?

In your workbook, list all of the ways your OCD costs you. Think about the impact of your OCD on these areas of your life:

- work: productivity, quality of working life, concentration, potential promotions, finding a more desirable position/ salary, relationships with coworkers, relationship with your boss

- relationship with your partner (if applicable): your partner's daily life and happiness, ability to be a supportive, loving partner, ability to spend mutually enjoyable time with your partner, ability to be emotionally supportive of your partner, overall quality of your relationship with your partner

- parental role (if applicable): ability to be emotionally supportive of your children, ability to set a good example for your children, ability to spend mutually enjoyable time with your children, overall quality of your relationship with your children

- social roles: ability to spend time with friends, ability to be emotionally supportive to friends, ability to spend mutually enjoyable time with friends, overall quality of your relationship with your friends

- personal development: ability to grow as a person, pursue your hobbies and interests, ability to serve your community or religious organization

WEIGHING AND BALANCING

The costs that you have just identified are real costs that you are currently experiencing. The concerns you may have about overcoming your OCD are about things that could potentially occur but may not. Furthermore, if they occur they may not last (anger from a spouse may let up over time, for example). So, you need to decide: do the costs of overcoming OCD truly, fully outweigh the costs of having it? If the answer is no, then this is probably not a good time in your life to make changes, and you may want to wait. If the answer is yes, then read on!

CHAPTER 7

The Paradox of Mental Control

INTRODUCTION

Having a sense of control is essential to achieving satisfaction, fulfillment, and security in life. All of us like to feel that we have control
over events in our lives, our daily activities, our work and leisure, and,
to a certain extent, our relationships. We also like to have a sense of
control over our behavior, emotions, thoughts, and bodily sensations.
That's why routines and predictability are so important; they help us
maintain a feeling of control. When we lose this sense of control, we
feel distressed and anxious. Similarly, loss of control over emotions
(unexpectedly bursting into tears), behavior (blurting out a comment
that you later regret), or body (a sudden, unexpected chest pain) are
upsetting. When you experience unwanted intrusive thoughts or
obsessions, part of your distress comes from the feeling of a loss of control over your mental faculties.

Danny was a devoutly religious married man who was plagued by
obsessional thoughts and images of having sex with people he associated with at work, and he thought that he had sinned in having such
thoughts. Danny tried various strategies to prevent the unwanted sexual thoughts from entering his mind, such as avoiding certain places or
people, and when a disturbing sexual thought intruded, he would try

to neutralize the thought by saying prayers. He would confess to his wife about having the thoughts, asking her to forgive him and reassure him that everything would be okay. Danny spent years engaged in a daily struggle to gain control over his unwanted intrusive sexual thoughts. He was convinced that he must be mentally weak. Like many people with OCD, he assumed that most "normal" people must be much better at controlling their unwanted thoughts and impulses than he was. After all, most people are not tortured daily by repeated disturbing thoughts, images, or impulses. But is it true that people in general have good control over their thoughts? Many people with OCD assume that others have much more control over their unwanted thoughts than they actually do. This chapter reviews what is known about control of thoughts and thought processes.

ATTENTION AND THOUGHTS

Recall that people have over 4,000 thoughts during waking hours of any given day. How do we manage to cope with such a large volume of mental activity? The answer lies in our attentional processes. We all have an attentional filter that guides which information, both internal (inside our heads) and external (from the environment around us), we turn our attention to and which information we ignore. Certain kinds of information take priority, such as information related to threat. For example, if your car is stalled on the railroad tracks and there is a train bearing down rapidly, your attention will be riveted on information relevant to your survival, such as undoing the seatbelt, unlocking the door, and running. It is unlikely that you would attend to information irrelevant to your survival, such as the music playing on the radio. If we didn't have this attentional filter, we would never have survived as a species.

We attend to thoughts that have relevance to our main goals and motives, both thoughts that promote those goals and motives and thoughts that may threaten those goals and motives. That is how we are able to manage the enormous volume of thoughts we experience on a regular basis; we ignore thoughts that are not relevant and we attend to those that are. Obsessional thoughts, of course, are thoughts that in some way threaten immediate goals and are highly distressing. As such, they receive full attentional priority, and it is extremely diffi-cult to ignore them. Indeed, ignoring an obsession is, for many people, akin to not attending to the train that is about to smash your car; that is, failing to pay attention to an obsession feels extremely dangerous and unwise. One reason for the persistence of your obsessions, then, is that they receive high attentional priority when they occur. One of the goals of this book is to help you recognize your obsessions as nonthreatening thoughts that do not require attention.

DELIBERATE ATTEMPTS TO CONTROL THOUGHTS

Although high attentional priority is one important factor in the persistence of obsessions, another critical factor is that people try so hard to control their obsessions. This is called the paradox of mental control; the harder people try to control a thought, the more difficulty they have with it.

FOCUS EXERCISE 7.1: THE "WHITE BEAR" TEST

Dr. Daniel Wegner (1994b) of Harvard University developed the "white bear" experiment to investigate our ability to control unwanted thoughts. Dr. Mark Freeston introduced a variation on the white bear test specifically for people with OCD (Freeston and Ladouceur 1999).

> The paradox of mental control is
> the harder people try to control a thought,
> the more difficulty they have with it.

Give it a try for yourself before we tell you what the research says about your ability to control thoughts.

1. Find a quiet room where you can sit comfortably without any interruptions. You will need your notebook, a pen, and a watch with a timer function.

2. Once you have these materials, start the experiment by closing your eyes and trying to think about white bears for two minutes.

3. Use the watch timer function to remind yourself when two minutes have passed.

4. You are to focus all of your mental ability on *keeping your mind focused on white bears*. However, if your mind does slip off the topic of white bears, make a mark in your notebook and try to refocus on the white bear theme.

5. After two minutes, stop the experiment and count up the marks. How did you do? How many times did your mind stray from the topic?

Most people are quite surprised at how hard it is to keep their mind focused on a single thought, even for a brief time period. Even with considerable mental effort and determination, few people are able to sustain their attention on a single idea. Here's an exercise that will help you learn more about how your thought processes work:

1. Give yourself a couple of minutes to relax but keep your notebook, pen, and watch handy.

2. Now close your eyes and try *not to think about white bears* for two minutes.

3. Make a mark in your notebook whenever the thought of white bears enters your mind.

4. If your mind does slip back to white bears, immediately try to suppress the thought after recording its occurrence in your notebook.

It is almost impossible to achieve perfect suppression of any unwanted thought, image, or impulse, even for a few minutes.

5. After two minutes, stop the thought suppression exercise. Count the number of marks recorded in your notebook.

6. How did you do? How difficult was it to keep white bears out of your mind?

7. Write down your immediate reactions to this experiment in your notebook for future reference. Did you expect to do better at suppressing your thoughts? How hard was it to control your thoughts? What did you learn from this exercise about mental control?

RESEARCH ON MENTAL CONTROL

Numerous studies have examined the impact of deliberate attempts to control, or suppress, thoughts. These studies have examined people with no psychological problems, as well as people who suffer from anxiety and mood problems, including OCD. Some of this work suggests that when people suppress a thought, they have some short-term success, but that after they stop trying, the thought returns with greater frequency. Other studies have found that suppression leads to an immediate increase in thought frequency. The exact effects of thought suppression on the frequency of thoughts are still a matter of debate among psychologists, but one thing has been clear throughout the dozens of studies published on thought suppression: it is almost impossible to achieve perfect suppression of any unwanted thought, image, or impulse, even for a few minutes.

If it is so difficult to rid the mind of a silly thought like "white bears," imagine how hard it is to not think about something that is terribly important or something that is associated with dire

> Despite people's best efforts at mental control, obsessions return with a vengeance. The harder people try to suppress an obsession, the more quickly it returns.

consequences. Imagine what would happen if you were fined $100 every time the white bear thought reoccurred, or you tried to suppress the thought over twenty minutes or two hours. Despite people's best efforts at mental control, obsessions return with a vengeance. The harder people try to suppress an obsession, the more quickly it returns.

WHY THE PARADOX?

Wegner (1994a) reports that intentional suppression of thoughts actually leads to an increase in those thoughts once people stop suppressing them. In describing his original thought suppression experiment, Wegner (1994b) noted that university students who previously suppressed white bear thoughts became unusually preoccupied with white bears over time. The very act of trying to control a thought led to an opposite, unintended effect; suppression can actually cause more preoccupation with an unwanted thought.

Wegner (1994a) has an interesting explanation for this paradoxical effect of mental control. He argues that mental control requires both a search for the thought that is to be suppressed and a search for distracters to get the mind off the thought that is to be suppressed should it occur. For example, if you do not want to have a sexual thought, your mind will be constantly monitoring itself for signs that the sexual thought is about to appear. At the same time, you will be deliberately thinking of thoughts that you can use to distract yourself from the sexual thought should it occur.

> The very act of trying to control a thought led to an opposite, unintended effect; suppression can actually cause more preoccupation with an unwanted thought.

FACTORS INFLUENCING THE SUCCESS OF MENTAL CONTROL

Searching for distracters takes a lot of mental effort, and your ability to effectively do so is really reduced when you have to concentrate on something else. However, your mind will keep scanning itself for signs of the thought you want to suppress, whether you have a distracter thought ready or not. What also happens is that all the distracters you used to replace the unwanted thought become associated with it and begin to actually trigger it. For example, during the white bear test, if you tried to suppress the white bear thought by replacing it with a thought of, say, a bluebird, eventually the thought of a bluebird will trigger the white bear thought.

Wegner (1994a) predicts that mental control can be successful when the two processes work together efficiently. This can only happen when your mental resources are not taxed. When your mental resources are stretched to their limits, such as when you have to concentrate on complex tasks, or when you are under stress or time pressure, it is much more difficult to keep unwanted thoughts away. Furthermore, it is difficult to suppress a negative thought if you are in a negative or distressing mood because the process that searches for distracters for that thought is more likely to find other negative distracters, which quickly remind you of the thought you are trying to suppress! Meanwhile, when your efforts at control fail, you become more distressed, and mental control becomes even more difficult. Finally, although you may be able to control your thoughts in the short term, there is evidence that our ability to exercise mental control over longer periods of time (i.e., hours) is quite poor. It is likely that you simply cannot sustain the consistent effort required to control a thought and continue with your daily life.

In summary, it is harder to control your thoughts under the following conditions:

- when you are trying to suppress them over a long time period

- when you are in an anxious or depressed mood state

- when you have to concentrate on a number of tasks besides suppressing the thoughts

> Individuals with OCD are often trying to control their obsessions under the very conditions in which thought control is most likely to fail.

The very worst conditions for trying to keep a thought at bay are when you are feeling pressured, distressed, or torn by competing demands. Unfortunately, these are the very conditions that describe the daily life of people suffering from OCD. Individuals with OCD are often trying to control their obsessions under the very conditions in which thought control is most likely to fail.

CONSEQUENCES OF FAILED MENTAL CONTROL

Clearly we all have lots of experience with failing in our efforts to get rid of an annoying or disturbing thought. What is the impact of this repeated failure? One result is an increase in distress, frustration, and depressed mood. In a study conducted by one of the authors, people with OCD sat quietly and monitored their most upsetting obsession. They tried very hard to suppress their obsessions, and yet not one person was able to achieve perfect suppression. This failure to achieve perfect control over the obsession was associated with an increase in negative appraisal of the obsession; that is, the more the thought returned while people were trying to suppress it, the more they believed that the thought was meaningful, harmful, or dangerous, and the harder they tried to control it. Furthermore, the more they had the thought while trying to suppress it, the more negative their mood state (Purdon, Rowa, and Antony 2005).

We are only beginning to research the impact that a negative appraisal of your failure to control unwanted thoughts might have in the escalation of obsessional thinking (Clark 2004). One thing is clear: a vicious cycle can develop in which the person tries harder and harder to control the obsession because of concerns over the consequences of failing to control it but only ends up creating conditions that further reduce the chance of successful mental control.

One thing is clear; a vicious cycle can develop in which the person tries harder and harder to control the obsession because of concerns over the consequences of failing to control it but only ends up creating conditions that further reduce the chance of successful mental control.

Kiran had repeated thoughts that serious harm or injury would come to her father or boyfriend whenever they were away from her. These thoughts upset her to the point that she engaged in compulsive checking, repeating, and mental neutralization rituals. For Kiran, failure to control these harm and injury obsessions was serious because she believed that the obsessions would increase the likelihood of harm occurring to her loved ones. She also believed that failure to control the obsessions would eventually cause her to become overwhelmed with anxiety and guilt. For Kiran, control of these obsessions was extremely important.

EFFECTIVENESS OF MENTAL CONTROL STRATEGIES

We know that people use a variety of strategies for managing their obsessions (Freeston and Ladouceur 1997). These include mental or behavioral distraction, rationalization, reassuring yourself or seeking reassurance from others, replacing the obsession with a positive thought, saying "stop," relaxation, self-questioning, self-punishment, analyzing the thought, or engaging in a mental or behavioral compulsion. Strategies that tend to be associated with higher frequency, return of the obsession, and more distress include the following:

- self-punishment (blaming yourself for the obsession)

- saying "stop" in response to the obsession

- compulsive ritual or neutralization

- worrying about having the obsession

We know from research that individuals with OCD tend to use these more problematic strategies. Purdon, Rowa, and Antony (working paper) found that the most commonly used strategy for controlling obsessions was saying "stop!" and that, in most cases, thought-suppression attempts were followed by use of a neutralizing strategy or compulsive act.

THWARTING THE PARADOX

No doubt your goal in reading this book is to find out how to reduce, if not eliminate, the suffering you experience from repetitive obsessions. That is, your goal is to get rid of obsessions. Yet we are telling you that trying to get rid of them actually makes the problem worse. How can you get rid of obsessional thinking, then? The key to overcoming the obsession is to abandon the belief that it has to be controlled. That is, the key is to begin to understand that the obsession is benign. There are three routes to this:

Deflate its significance. One of the most important differences between people with obsessions and those without obsessions is that individuals with obsessions pay more attention to their unwanted intrusive thoughts, evaluate them as being more important, and are more likely to believe they must control their thoughts to prevent some dreaded consequence. Exercises that lead to a more balanced view of the threat represented by the obsession will lead to a reduction in its frequency and persistence. Chapters 8 and 9 describe exercises that can assist you in deflating the significance of your obsessions.

Exposure. One of the most powerful strategies for gaining control over an obsession is to intentionally expose yourself to it. Chapter 10 will describe this more fully, but suffice it to say that intentionally holding on to the obsession goes a long way toward robbing it of its significance and the fear it induces.

Reduce stress. You will have more success in controlling unwanted intrusive thoughts if you are not depressed, anxious, stressed, or overwhelmed with competing demands. Chapter 11 assists you with stress management.

CHAPTER 8

Overcoming Obsessions with Themes of Harm, Violence, and Sex

VIOLENT AND SEXUAL OBSESSIONS

Violent and sexual obsessions are often alarming in ways that other kinds of obsessions are not. For example, people whose obsessions concern cleanliness, germs, and dirt may feel that their concerns are exaggerated, but they are not typically alarmed that they would have such concerns in the first place. People who have thoughts of harming loved ones or sexually exploiting innocent people are typically alarmed by the fact that they would have such thoughts to begin with. These thoughts go against morals, values, and personality to a greater extent than do other kinds of obsessions. Part of the key to overcoming thoughts of this type is acceptance of the thoughts and the recognition that thoughts like this can happen to anyone; that is, you do not have to be a murderer or a pedophile to experience these thoughts. Note that acceptance does not mean liking or condoning such thoughts, but rather accepting that they are a phenomenon that many people experience. This chapter will introduce some exercises that will help you "de-catastrophize" what it means to have repugnant obsessions. There are a number of exercises in this chapter, one of which requires a week of monitoring. Others can be done right away. Thus, this chapter will take a couple of weeks to get through.

WHAT ARE YOUR APPRAISALS?

In chapter 4, you worked hard to determine the kind of appraisal that was causing your distress over your obsessions. Before reading further, go back to Focus Exercise 4.2 and review the kinds of ways you appraise your obsessional thoughts. Your appraisals likely fall into the categories described in chapter 3: inflated responsibility, overestimation of threat, thought-action fusion, mental control, intolerance of uncertainty, or perfectionism. Obsessions involving harm, violence, and sexual themes most commonly give rise to inflated responsibility, thought-action fusion, and mental control. These are the kinds of appraisals that this chapter will focus on. The goal is to help you identify your incorrect appraisal of your obsessions and develop a more accurate view of what they mean.

THOUGHT-ACTION FUSION

Richard, from Focus Exercise 4.1, was fairly certain he was not a pedophile; he had never had any desire whatsoever to be involved with a child sexually, had never fantasized about such activity, and enjoyed a healthy sexual relationship with his wife. The idea of engaging in a sexual act with a child was wholly repugnant and the idea of harming a child in this or any way went against every fiber of his being. He had undergone a thorough assessment by experts, who had concluded that he was not a pedophile. However, Richard was afraid that having these thoughts meant that he was actually a pedophile but hadn't realized it yet, and therefore hadn't started acting on it yet (hence the assessment hadn't picked it up). He believed that if he continued to have the thoughts he might snap and act on them. Like Daphne in Focus Exercise 4.2, Richard believed that having the thoughts was the moral equivalent of actually acting on them.

Daphne was plagued by impulses to kick or trip people on the street, especially people who were vulnerable, such as elderly people, mothers carrying babies, or people walking with crutches or canes. Daphne was known by her friends and family to be a gentle, caring person, and she had never done anything remotely aggressive to another person or animal ever in her life. She was sickened by these impulses, especially since she was studying to be a nurse. Daphne felt that it was just as bad, morally, to be having such thoughts as it was to actually kick and trip people. She assumed that these thoughts must be revealing another side to her, a side she didn't realize she had. She believed that if she kept having such thoughts, she might eventually snap and act on them. Daphne also wondered if the thoughts were a sign that she was going to commit acts of harm in the future and should therefore not pursue a career in a helping profession.

Gaining Perspective

This section is relevant for people who experience obsessional impulses or urges. If you do not have impulses or urges, it may not apply to you. It is true that thinking about an action is often the first step in engaging in that action. However, it is *not* true that having a thought about an action always leads to that action. Think about your own activities in the past few days. It is likely that there have been numerous times that you thought about doing something that you didn't end up doing. For example, you might have been sitting at your desk spying a box of doughnuts by the coffee machine and thought about getting one but didn't. You might have thought about stopping to pick up a movie on the way home but didn't. You might have thought about really letting into a rude salesperson but didn't. The list of examples is endless. The point is that the link between thoughts and actions is indirect; there are numerous factors that determine whether or not you carry a thought about an action into an action.

> The link between thoughts and actions is indirect;
> there are numerous factors that determine whether
> or not you carry a thought about an action into an action.

The idea of an action occurs fairly suddenly but so do our thoughts about the pros and cons of engaging in that action at a particular time. You may have a thought of taking a doughnut, but then you think about the calories and cholesterol and decide against taking one. You may decide that you are too tired for a movie, and you may decide that it is not worth the aggravation to involve yourself in a conflict with a salesperson.

You may have read that people can "act on impulse," behaving in ways they later regret. That certainly is true; there are people who act without considering the consequences. However, the actions such people engage in are actions that they enjoy or are desirable in the moment, such as shopping or gambling or yelling at someone they are angry with. They may regret the action later because of its consequences, but in the moment, the idea is quite attractive. Now think about your obsessional urges. Are they activities that give you pleasure at any level? If not, then in order to act on the thought, you have to go against what you enjoy doing, in addition to going against your morals and values. This makes it far more unlikely that you will act on your obsession. You may be concerned that you will start to find your obsessions enjoyable at some level. It is possible, but highly improbable; adults' personalities, morals, and values are generally consistent and stable over time. It would take a truly radical identity shift for someone who abhors violence and exploitation to engage in it.

You may also be thinking of times when you did lose control of your behavior and are concerned that this means you are capable of losing control over any kind of behavior in any circumstance. It is important to keep in mind that everyone feels that he or she has lost control over his or her behavior at some point in time, but, in fact, people usually retain considerable control. For example, even the most loving mother can lose her temper and speak in an unnecessarily harsh manner to her child. Yet even at her angriest, she does not hit the child. Even the calmest motorist can be galled into making an inappropriate hand gesture to a car that cuts him off, but even at his angriest, he does not leave his car to physically confront the driver. Both of these people would report being "out of control" of their behavior because they had engaged in behaviors they don't like; however, even at their most "uncontrolled," their actions do not deviate very far from their morals and values. Furthermore, recall that the experience of unwanted, unacceptable thoughts about engaging in harm, violence, or sexually exploitative acts is quite common. If having such thoughts led to action, the jails would be bursting at the seams.

The next exercise is designed to help you develop an accurate, objective perspective on the probability of you acting on your obsessional thoughts.

FOCUS EXERCISE 8.1: TRY TO MAKE YOURSELF LOSE CONTROL OVER YOUR BEHAVIOR

Think of an action that you could actually do but would really not want to do, such as the following:

- yelling something out loud at a grocery store

- singing out loud at a bus stop or in an elevator

- jumping up and down while waiting in a line (when it is not cold)

There may be an action that you have already thought of doing or been tempted to do but don't because it is highly undesirable. Do not choose an action that you are highly concerned about (that is, don't choose one of your obsessions). Instead, choose an undesirable act that you don't think about doing very often and one where the only person who could be "harmed" is you. Write about the action in detail in your notebook. Rate how likely you are to engage in that action. Now, for the next week, think about that activity as hard and as often as you can. Imagine where you would do it and how. Read your description of the action several times a day if you can, and try to think of it whenever you can. You may want to give yourself a reminder to do this, such as wearing your watch on your other wrist. At the end of the week, write down how often you actually did engage in the action. Rate again how likely you think you are to do it now.

Gaining Perspective

Daphne was concerned that the persistence of her thought about kicking or tripping people might be a kind of premonition. There is a religious tradition according to which God communicates to people by giving them signs. If you feel that your thoughts could be a sign from God, you should speak with your spiritual advisor for guidance in understanding what your thoughts might mean. There is also a superstitious tradition according to which thoughts (and dreams) can be premonitions. People will speak widely of their dreams that bear out, and their stories are often repeated. However, it is important to recognize that for every dream that comes true, there are thousands that do not; most people report having at most a handful of experiences in their lifetime in which their dreams or "premonitions," in the form of thoughts, were born out, yet the average person has several dreams per night, and thousands of thoughts per day. Dreams and thoughts, then, are unlikely to be the best source of information on which to base important decisions. Daphne wondered if she should change careers as a result of her thoughts. But would it be rational for her to discount all of the factors that led her to choose a career in nursing (her interest, caring, and compassion, the salary, how well she is suited to the hours a nurse works) for the sake of her superstition? A much better explanation for the recurrence of obsessions is presented later in this chapter, in the section on appraisals of thoughts and thought control (also see chapter 7).

Gaining Perspective

Another aspect of thought-action fusion is the idea that having a thought about an immoral deed is the moral equivalent of actually doing that deed. Daphne and Richard believed that they were terrible people and morally corrupt for having the kinds of thoughts that they had. Is this an accurate view? Consider the following. There are some religious traditions that would consider it sinful or immoral to have a thought about an immoral deed, even an unbidden one. Many religious traditions do, however, take the involuntary nature of a thought into account. For example, a spontaneous thought about an immoral deed would not be considered sinful or immoral, whereas an actively generated fantasy about engaging in a sexual act with another person's spouse would.

It is also important to keep in mind that your repugnant obsessions are not the sum total of your morality. Think of someone you view as being virtuous and moral. What informs your sense of their morality? Chances are it is their actions. If you were to learn that this person was plagued by unwanted, unacceptable thoughts about immoral actions, to what extent would it change your overall view of their morality? Former President Jimmy Carter, who is celebrated as a man of moral integrity for his dedication to world peace and acts of charity, confessed that he had committed adultery in his mind but had never and would never commit such an act. The same rules apply to you; your morality is much more than your thoughts.

FOCUS EXERCISE 8.2: IMMORALITY IN PERSPECTIVE

In your notebook, write down the name of the most virtuous person you know, either from your own life or from the media. Now write down the most immoral person you know, either personally or from the media. Also consider the difference between having a thought about an action and committing an action. Think about people you know from the newspaper or TV who have committed acts of murder or sexual exploitation. Now think about the worst criminal in history. Now list several of your best friends and closest family members. Draw a line down the page. Write the name of the most virtuous at the top of the line and the person who is the most criminal at the bottom of the line. Now place everyone else on the line according to how moral they are, overall. Now put yourself on the line.

Now reconsider whether the fact that you experience thoughts about immoral acts truly makes you immoral.

Taking Educated Risks

You may find it temporarily reassuring to read that we don't seem to think you are going to act on your impulses, that you did not act on an impulse you thought about all week, and that your morality

This is Richard's line:

⊤ *Most Virtuous*	
┼ Mother Theresa	
┼ Laurie Ashraf	
┼ George Bai	
┼ ME	
┼ Jennifer	
┼ Michael	
┼ Clifford Olsen*	*serial killer who has held at least 10 children captive, repeatedly assaulting them sexually before killing them*
┼ Stalin	
⊥ *Most Criminal*	

is determined by factors other than your obsessions. However, the goal here is not to give you reassurance but rather to help you recognize that the realistic probability of acting on your obsessions is low enough that you can risk going about your daily activities without needing to protect anyone from the harm represented by them. If you feel that you must organize your life to prevent harm, even when the probability of that harm is very small, then you will want to pay particular attention to the section on responsibility appraisals below.

Responsibility Appraisals

Recall that responsibility appraisals reflect the ideas that

- failing to prevent harm is as bad, morally, as actually causing harm, and

- if you have any influence over a negative outcome whatsoever, then you are fully responsible for doing whatever you can to prevent that outcome, no matter how tiny the probability of that negative outcome is.

Natalia was driving past a crosswalk one day and felt her car drive over something on the road. She looked in the rearview mirror and saw a pothole. A little while later, she suddenly wondered if she had in fact run over someone without realizing it. This concern began to plague her whenever she drove. She kind of knew it was highly unlikely that she would be able to hit someone and not realize it, but she felt that as long as there was a possibility she could do so, she was honor bound to investigate and help the potential victim. As a result, she often retraced her route, looking for people lying in the road or on the shoulders, and eventually even the ditches. Natalia felt that to not check like this was akin to actually murdering people.

Isabelle found preparing meals for her family to be highly stressful, particularly after her elderly aunt moved into the home. She was terrified that she might inadvertently poison her family by failing to prepare food hygienically. Before opening a can, she would check the expiration date and search the can for any dents or imperfections. She would sterilize the lid and the can opener before opening the can. Isabelle recognized that without taking such precautions the probability that she might inadvertently expose her family to botulism or salmonella was quite low, but, like Natalia, she felt that as long as the probability of causing harm was not zero, she needed to take extreme precautions to prevent harm; to not take such elaborate precautions was, in her view, the same as actively poisoning her family.

Gaining Perspective

Natalia, Isabelle, and Richard have an exaggerated view of their responsibility to others. They know intellectually that the probability that they will cause harm is fairly low, but feel they must defend

> The realistic probability of acting on your obsessions is low enough that you can risk going about your daily activities without needing to protect anyone from the harm represented by them.

against harm at all costs. As a result, they organize their lives around preventing events that have a fairly low probability of occurring. Now examine this. Most people do not go to extreme lengths to prevent an outcome of minute probability from occurring. Why not? Because the vast majority of people take educated, or calculated risks. Most people will take such precautions as ensuring that their young children are immunized and washing their hands after using the toilet, before preparing or eating food, and after handling raw meat. They take such precautions because the odds of harm occurring are high enough to justify taking them. Daphne, who is training to be a nurse, does need to take careful precautions. However, Daphne is not able to accept the precautions recommended by her supervisors, and instead, she engages in precautions to such an extent that she actually isn't an effective caregiver. One of the main differences between people with OCD and people without OCD is that people without OCD are willing to act using the balance of probabilities as a guide; if the risk of harm is very small, then the cost of taking precautions outweighs the perceived benefits. If the risk of harm is higher, people without OCD are able to use accepted standards to guide their precautionary actions, whereas those with OCD cannot.

Imagine if everyone in the world felt the same degree of responsibility to protect others from harm as Natalia, Isabelle, and Daphne do. People might be safer, but harm would still occur, for it would be impossible to anticipate and effectively defend against all harm. Meanwhile, the world would grind to a halt. People could no longer focus their energies on growing crops, trading stock, running government, teaching, and so on.

FOCUS EXERCISE 8.3: DO THE POTENTIAL BENEFITS JUSTIFY ORGANIZING YOUR LIFE AROUND PREVENTION?

Refer to Focus Exercise 6.3, where you identified the costs of OCD. Ask yourself, is it *rational* to jeopardize your most valued relationships, your job, and/or your personal life, in order to attempt to prevent events that have a minute probability of occurring? Now ask yourself, is it *fair* to yourself and to the important people in your life to jeopardize your most valued relationships, your job, and/or your personal life, in order to attempt to prevent events that have a minute probability of occurring? You have a right to your own life, and the important people in your life want you to have your own life.

Gaining Perspective

Is failing to prevent harm the moral equivalent of causing harm? Isabelle and Richard certainly thought so. This issue is similar to the issue of thoughts about an immoral act being equivalent to committing an immoral act. Let's consider.

FOCUS EXERCISE 8.4:
ACTS OF OMISSION VS. COMMISSION

In your notebook, write down all of the ways you attempt to prevent harm from coming as a result of your obsession. These can include compulsions, avoidance, and neutralizing. Now, as in Focus Exercise 8.2, we are going to plot different things on a line ranging from "highly moral" at one end of the line to "wholly immoral" at the other end. Rather than plotting people's names on the line, you are going to plot actions and inactions. First, draw a line down a page in your notebook. Think of the worst possible action you can imagine someone doing and write it at the bottom of the line. Now think of the best possible action you can imagine someone doing, and write it at the top of the line. Now write on the line where *not* doing each of your avoidance, neutralizing, and coping responses would fall in relation to most and least moral events. As you do this exercise, keep a realistic perspective on the actual degree of threat your obsessions pose. If you haven't done the previous exercises, go back and do them first. You can use several lines if you have a lot of items to plot. Here is one of the lines that Daphne, who had thoughts of harming elderly and vulnerable people, wrote:

Highly Moral

Putting my life at risk to save someone else

Not checking when I think I might have spilled water

Murdering a child

Wholly Immoral

The point of this exercise is to help you appreciate that there is a vast difference between actively causing harm and failing to act to prevent a harmful event of low probability.

Appraisals About Thoughts and Thought Control

Daphne and Richard didn't understand why their thoughts kept returning even though they tried hard not to have them and didn't want to have them. The following discussion is meant to help you gain a better understanding of why your obsessions keep occurring, despite your best efforts. The primary reasons your obsessions keep returning are that

- you are preoccupied with not having them, so they are ironically always on your mind, ready to pop up to the surface

- although you have tried hard not to have them, you have spent considerable time thinking about your obsessions in your attempts to understand them; thus they have become a major current concern, just as food is to a dieter

- you are on the lookout for them, and so you have become highly sensitive to anything that is associated with them, including situations, sights, sounds, colors, people, relevant information in the media, and feelings (anger, anxiety, frustration, fear, hopelessness)

Gaining Perspective

Again, people actually have fairly limited control over their thoughts; however, knowing this is true is not necessarily believing it. The following exercise is meant to help you gain a better understanding of your own thought processes.

FOCUS EXERCISE 8.5: IDENTIFYING THE LIMITS OF YOUR CONTROL OVER THOUGHTS

Part I: You need a watch with a second hand for this part of the exercise. Visualize the following: a white miniature poodle wearing a red bow and a black-and-pink polka dot bikini. Form the image in your mind as vividly as you can. Concentrate on that image for the next sixty seconds. After sixty seconds, bring that image to mind again and hold it for another sixty seconds. Write a description of that image in your notebook. Now, get rid of the thought; erase it completely from your mind. Now, for the next forty-eight hours you are *not* to have any thoughts about poodles wearing red bows and black-and-pink polka dot bikinis. You must try your hardest not to have such thoughts. Complete the next part of this exercise after forty-eight hours have passed.

Part II: How successful were you at erasing the image? What did you notice about thought recurrences? Did you find that the image was triggered by the colors red, black, and pink? Did you find that the image was triggered by seeing dogs or seeing your notebook or seeing this book? Did you find that over the course of the forty-eight hours, the range of things that triggered the thoughts became larger and more general (that at the beginning, the thought might be triggered by seeing a poodle, but at the end, it was triggered just by seeing a dog)? The same processes that made it difficult for you to control this image have made it difficult for you to control your obsessions. These processes are not unique to OCD; what is unique to OCD is not the ability to control thoughts but the degree of investment in controlling them!

MAKING USE OF THIS INFORMATION

This chapter has given you a considerable amount of information about thoughts and thought processes. Again, our goal here is not to reassure you; our goal is to enable you to take educated risks with your obsessions by not engaging in your compulsions, neutralizing, and avoidance. You may find that you feel better now when you have read this chapter, but that the moment the obsession occurs later on, this information will be of no use to you. You need to be able to use this information in the moment!

FOCUS EXERCISE 8.6: MODIFYING INCORRECT APPRAISALS OF YOUR OBSESSIONS IN THE MOMENT

This exercise is the same as what you did in Focus Exercise 4.2, except this time there is a fifth column, entitled "balanced appraisal." Greenberger and Padesky (1995), who are experts in helping people cope with negative thoughts, use this term to describe appraisals that take into account all the information about a subject, not just the information that springs to mind or is noticed when you are anxious or distressed. Once every morning, afternoon, and evening for the next week, record your obsession, the feelings it evokes, and your immediate appraisal. But then, reconsider that immediate appraisal in light of all the information provided in this book, so far. That is, come up with an appraisal that takes into account your new understanding of thoughts and thought processes, as well as responsibility, morality, and harm. Then, rate the intensity of your feelings again. This is a page from Daphne's chart.

Date	Obsession	Feelings	Immediate Appraisal	Balanced Appraisal
Feb. 12-morn.	Impulse to kick out the crutch of an injured person	Fear-90 Shame-80	Am I a psychopath?? I wouldn't be having thoughts like this unless part of me truly wanted to do it. Should I be changing careers? The more I have these thoughts the more likely I am to act on them! I am a menace to society. I am a bad person for having these thoughts.	I might be a psychopath, but the probability that I am is low enough that I don't need to take precautions to protect people from me. These thoughts may be a sign that I should change careers, but more reliable information suggests that for now this is an excellent career choice. I am a moral person overall, because I do many good works in the community and do not harm or exploit anyone; even a person like me can have thoughts like this. Fear-30 Shame-20
Feb. 12-aft.	What if some water spilled onto the floor from the drinking fountain, and someone slipped and hurt themselves?	Fear-80 Guilt-90	I don't think any water spilled, but maybe it did, and if anything happened it would be all my fault. Not going back to clean up any water is just like actually tripping someone.	It is possible I spilled water on the floor; however, the probability is low enough that the cost of being late for my class is greater than the potential gain of returning to the fountain. There is a really big difference between tripping someone deliberately and not checking if there is water on the floor when you're pretty sure there isn't. Fear-10 Guilt-15

Feb. 12- even.	Urge to trip elderly person	Fear-90 Guilt-90 Shame-90	I am a bad person. These thoughts keep happening, even though I don't want them to! They must be a sign of something; maybe I want to do it; maybe I am a cold, callous person at heart and this is a sign that I shouldn't go into nursing. I'm going to lose control and do it. Not controlling this thought is the same as actually tripping someone.	I have no history of violent or aggressive behavior; even though I have these urges, I have a choice as to whether I act on them. There is a big difference between having thoughts like this and actually hurting someone; they are not the same thing at all. Fear-20 Guilt-20 Shame-15

TAKING THE PLUNGE: EXPOSURE

By gradually phasing out your compulsions, neutralizing, and avoidance, the goal of this chapter was to help you prepare to take acceptable risks. You may now be fully able and willing to take educated, calculated risks and be ready to plunge into exposure; if so, go for it! Even if you still doubt that such risks are educated and calculated, we highly recommend that you begin exposure now; sometimes, you can talk about something over and over again, and it doesn't hit home, but taking the plunge does. You may be the kind of person who needs the experience of taking risks before your appraisal of your obsessions changes. Finally, you may be starting to use this new information as a form of compulsion or neutralizing; that is, when you get the obsession, you may review the information as a means of reducing your anxiety and find that you feel better for a while. This will not help you in the long run and, in fact, may make your OCD worse. You must put the information to the test by actually taking the risks. The longer you avoid doing exposure, the longer you will have your OCD.

> You must put the information to the test by actually taking the risks. The longer you avoid doing exposure, the longer you will have your OCD.

CHAPTER 9

Religious Obsessions and Compulsions

INTRODUCTION

Dominic was a devout middle-aged fundamentalist Christian who brought her religious beliefs to bear on every aspect of her life. In her mid-forties, she developed a life-threatening illness that confined her to bed and caused her to think more concretely about her afterlife. Dominic became increasingly preoccupied with whether she had committed a sin, whether God would punish her with eternal damnation, and whether she had made the right decision that was pleasing to God. Dominic would repeat prayers of confession and praise to God and would look for signs (reassurance) in sermons or Christian songs that she had made correct decisions or had pleased God. She incessantly searched Scripture for verses that would allay her doubts, and she would accost friends and family with the same question over and over again: "Do you think I have displeased God?" Whatever their answer, it would never satisfy Dominic. Within minutes, she could destroy their reassurance with a twisted logic that began with "but what if . . ."

By the time that Dominic was referred for treatment of OCD, her entire day was spent in tormented doubt over sin and punishment and she found it difficult to make decisions even about basic hygiene because she was afraid she might displease God. Ciarrocchi (1995) notes that an overly sensitive moral conscience can interfere with faith. Famous religious figures who have suffered with religious obsessions and compulsions include John Bunyan, who wrote *Pilgrim's Progress*, St. Ignatius Loyola, founder of the Jesuits, and possibly Martin Luther, the Protestant reformer.

RELIGIOUS DIVERSITY

This chapter is intended for devoutly religious people of all faiths. We approach religious obsessions and compulsions not as a theological problem but as a manifestation of a psychological disorder called OCD. If you are having difficulty applying this chapter to your religious tradition, it may be helpful to seek the counsel of a spiritual guide of your faith, who can work with you on the application of this chapter to your religious struggles.

DOES RELIGION CAUSE OCD?

Are people of faith more likely to suffer from OCD? There is no evidence that religion causes OCD. However, your religious background and experience can influence the type of obsessional concerns that develop in people with OCD. Culture has an impact on the content of obsessional symptoms. For example, in countries where religious education and practice are expressed in laws and cultural norms, there tend to be higher levels of religious obsessions (Steketee, Quay, and White 1991).

RELIGIOUS DEVOTION: HOW MUCH IS TOO MUCH?

Theologians and religious scholars throughout the ages have recognized that scrupulosity is "an illness of the mind" that must not be

> There is no evidence that religion causes OCD. However, your religious background and experience can influence the type of obsessional concerns that develop in people with OCD.

confused for strong religious devotion. Over the centuries, Christian theologians have recognized that scrupulosity arises out of fear and an erroneous conscience. Therefore, the religious person suffering from obsessional doubt cannot use his or her conscience when making moral judgments or decisions (Ciarrocchi 1995). Greenberg (1984) notes that Jewish codes of law explicitly state that you should not worry about minor violations of your Passover cleaning once it is complete, and particular lines or sections of the liturgy should never be repeated. The Islamic scholar, Said Nursi, makes an insightful observation about scrupulosity that is entirely consistent with a cognitive behavioral approach to OCD:

> O one afflicted with the sickness of scruples! Do you know what your scruples resemble? A calamity! The more importance they are given, the more they grow. If you give them no importance, they die away. If you see them as big, they grow bigger. If you see them as small, they grow smaller. If you fear them, they swell and make you ill. If you do not fear them, they are light and remain hidden. (Nursi 1998)

If your religious devotion impairs, rather than enhances, your spiritual life and other aspects of your life, then it has crossed the line.

FAULTY APPRAISALS AND BELIEFS

We previously discussed the kinds of intrusive thoughts about sin, punishment, and doubt that plague the person suffering from religious obsessions and compulsions. All religious people sometimes have thoughts about whether they have committed a sin, whether they are truly repentant, or whether they have performed a religious ritual correctly. The devout believer is able to evaluate these doubts in a rational manner and determine whether some corrective response is needed. The scrupulous person, on the other hand, falls prey to a number of incorrect appraisals that lead to the erroneous conclusion that having such doubt is highly significant. The appraisals most relevant to religious obsessions are thought-action fusion, perfectionism, intolerance of uncertainty, and control over thoughts.

You should have developed a good understanding of the kind of appraisals that play a role in your OCD from doing Focus Exercise 4.1 and Focus Exercise 4.2. It is absolutely critical that you complete these exercises before engaging in the treatment recommendations discussed below. You need to clearly specify your main religious obsessions, their frequency, level of emotional distress, how they are appraised, and how you typically respond to the obsession (compulsion, neutralization). This information is needed to tailor this book's treatment recommendations to your OCD and to assess whether you are making progress as you engage in the treatment exercises.

The next sections will help you overcome your religious obsessions by challenging the meaning you currently give them, but first, a caveat: Ciarrocchi (1995) notes that a belief unique to the person with scruples is ". . . that the therapy tasks themselves may in some way be wrong from a moral or religious standpoint" (p. 80). You may become anxious when reading the therapy exercises and strategies described below, thinking, "You are asking me to intentionally think an evil or impure thought," or "You are suggesting that I intentionally refrain from confessing my sins or reduce the time spent praying." If you are stuck on this point, we suggest that you discuss the exposure exercises and other behavioral experiments with a spiritual guide or pastoral counselor who understands OCD. He or she can give you advice on which exercises would not be a violation of your doctrinal standards and faith. In the meantime, we encourage you to read on and take a first step toward your own recovery from OCD. If you feel quite anxious even reading some of the examples used below, remember that these ideas are ours, not yours. You are reading our ideas, our thoughts, so to speak, not your own thoughts. You cannot take responsibility for what we have written.

CHALLENGING APPRAISALS

The first step in breaking the OCD cycle is to begin to challenge your appraisal of the meaning of your obsessional thoughts. Recall that there are various types of appraisals that apply to religious obsessions.

Thought-Action Fusion: Bad Thoughts Equal Bad Deeds

Most often, scrupulous individuals are engaged in a self-defeating struggle to gain better control over unwanted thoughts of sin, punishment, and blasphemy. The distress caused by this struggle is in part due to their belief that "bad thoughts are as immoral as bad actions," a bias that Dr. Rachman called "moral thought-action fusion" (TAF) (Rachman and Shafran 1999). Is it true that thoughts you consider bad, impure, or immoral are really the moral equivalent to some enactment of the thought?

Gaining Perspective

Focus Exercise 8.2 dealt with this problem of moral TAF as it relates to violent and aggressive obsessions. You can use this same technique to evaluate the legitimacy of this assumption in relation to matters of faith.

FOCUS EXERCISE 9.1: IMMORALITY IN PERSPECTIVE

The following is an example of Marie's "morality line."

Most Moral
Jesus
Mother Teresa
Billy Graham
Grandmother
Deacon in my church
Sue, my best friend
ME
My father
Friend who betrayed me
Murderer
Serial killer
Hitler
Most Immoral

In your notebook, draw a line and at one end write down the names of individuals you admire for their high moral character and at the other end of the line write down people you think are highly immoral. Between the two ends of the line write in the names of individuals you think possess varying degrees of morality and immorality. After you have done this, place yourself anywhere on the line that represents your own view of your moral worth. Would you place yourself closer to the moral or the immoral end?

Now review your morality chart and write down the reasons why you placed each of these individuals where you did on the morality line. What is it that made some individuals more moral than others?

There are two things that you can learn from this exercise. First, it is likely that you categorized individuals as moral or immoral based on their behavior more than on their thoughts or attitudes. When making judgments of other people's morality, you are more likely to base this on their behavior. After all, would you consider a person highly moral if she or he talked a lot about the importance of kindness toward others but never did anything for others and instead only looked out for himself or herself? Likewise, people may have unsavory thoughts, but you tend not to judge them as immoral until they engage in immoral behavior. Something else you can learn from the morality line is whether you are more biased toward assuming immorality in yourself than in others. Are you really only slightly more moral than a murderer or serial killer? Are you being biased, or overly harsh in your judgments of yourself? You can use the morality line to self-correct your own evaluation of your moral worth.

Another way to challenge the TAF moral bias is to examine the basis of your moral judgments. Are you assuming that all disgusting thoughts, images, or impulses are immoral? Most major religions of the world, including Christianity, make a distinction between unwanted, spontaneous, and distressing intrusive thoughts and

> Individuals with scrupulosity often overlook the functional significance of the thought, and so erroneously categorize their unwanted intrusive thoughts as impure or sinful.

deliberate, intentional thoughts. For example, Larry was plagued by blasphemous thoughts and impulses to "curse God." He was a devout Catholic and found these thoughts most distressing. He prayed continually for deliverance and regularly went to confession. Mike, on the other hand, was an atheist who had several negative experiences with religion during childhood and as an adult despised the Church. Mike often cursed the Church, God, and any form of organized religion. Although Mike and Larry had similar thoughts, there is a huge moral chasm between the two. The Church would consider Mike's thoughts impure and sinful because they represent an intentional denial of God. Larry's thoughts would not be considered impure or immoral because they are not wanted or intentional. Instead they are the symptom of a psychological illness called OCD. Individuals with scrupulosity often overlook the functional significance of the thought, and so erroneously categorize their unwanted intrusive thoughts as impure or sinful. After all, would you not agree that there is a big difference between accidentally running over a pedestrian and purposefully running down someone you intensely dislike who is walking along the side of the road?

This section discussed the faulty appraisal called moral TAF. If you believe that "bad" thoughts are equivalent to "bad" deeds, then you are likely to conclude that any thought, image, or impulse that is contrary to your religious or moral values is impure and sinful. However, we have argued that moral evaluations consider deeds as much more important than thoughts. Thus "bad" thoughts are not morally equivalent to "bad" deeds. In addition, whether or not a thought or image is impure depends on its function; that is, whether it is wanted and intended. By their very definition, obsessions cannot be immoral because they are unwanted, unintended, and highly distressing. Obsessions are a product of a psychological problem—OCD—and not a spiritual problem.

By their very definition, obsessions cannot be immoral because they are unwanted, unintended, and highly distressing. Obsessions are a product of a psychological problem—OCD—and not a spiritual problem.

FOCUS EXERCISE 9.2:
CHALLENGING MORAL TAF

Over the next week or two, use the charts outlined in Focus Exercise 4.1 and Focus Exercise 4.2 to practice challenging moral TAF beliefs. This can be done in your notebook. Try to catch yourself a few times each day when your primary religious obsession floods your mind. Write down in the appraisal column whether you are automatically thinking that the thought is highly immoral. Now use Focus Exercise 9.1 to challenge this belief. Recall your "morality line" and whether thoughts really are morally equivalent to deeds. Remind yourself that the obsession cannot be immoral, for it is unwanted and disturbing. Rather, these characteristics of the thought make the intrusion a symptom of OCD and not a spiritual or moral problem.

Moral Perfectionism

Another faulty belief in scrupulosity that is related to moral TAF is the assumption that you should strive for a perfect moral state. This is expressed in phrases like "trying to always please God," "trying to never make a wrong decision," or "trying to commit no sin."

Gaining Perspective

Are these goals possible to attain? Are there any negative consequences with having impossibly high personal moral goals? The following exercises are intended to test out moral perfectionistic strivings and to offer an alternative approach that might lead to less personal distress and suffering.

FOCUS EXERCISE 9.3:
PERFECTIONIST STRIVINGS RECORD

You can use this exercise to better understand your perfectionistic strivings and their effect on scrupulosity. In your notebook, make four columns. Label the first column "moral goals/values," the second column "ways to achieve moral goals/values," the third column "level of distress" during moral strivings, and the fourth column "level of success" in achieving moral goals. Use a rating scale of 0 to 100, where 0 is none and 100 is absolute. If you have trouble doing this exercise from memory, try completing it over a two-week period as you pay special attention to your moral perfectionistic strivings. The following is a sample of Bob's moral strivings record.

Moral Goals/Values	Ways to Achieve Moral Goals/Values	Level of Distress (0 to 100)	Level of Success (0 to 100)
1. Be totally honest in my interactions with others.	Repeat conversations to ensure complete honesty.	82	15
	Repeatedly question others to ensure I have not communicated a falsehood.	77	50
	Avoid social conversation to reduce the chances of spreading a falsehood.	15	87
2. Be certain that I've never taken what doesn't belong to me.	Go back into stores to ensure I didn't take something by mistake.	62	90
	Repeatedly check pockets, briefcase, etc. to ensure I haven't taken something by mistake.	71	84
	Repeatedly check when I leave a person's office to make sure I haven't taken pens, paper, etc.	90	22

It may be that you can identify five or six moral or religious values that are relevant to your OCD. After you've completed this perfectionist strivings record, review what you've just written. Are there certain values and practices that are more distressing than others? Are there certain practices that are less successful, despite your greatest efforts? Are some of these moral/faith values more central to your OCD than others? You will want to target for change those moral/faith values that are most distressing and most closely tied to your obsessions and compulsions.

You can also use your perfectionist strivings record to help you develop healthier, more realistic moral and religious values and practices. You could discuss your perfectionist strivings record with a spiritual guide or pastoral counselor to obtain some advice on whether your moral and religious goals are helpful or detrimental to your faith. What is your spiritual advisor's overall impression of your religious goals and values? How close do your goals and values match those advocated by your faith community? Does your spiritual guide think that your religious and moral goals are realistic and attainable? Does he or she think that these goals strengthen or weaken your faith? Does your spiritual advisor consider these goals and values an outgrowth of religious devotion or a symptom of OCD?

Two cautions about working with a spiritual guide on your moral perfectionism beliefs. First, it is very important that you complete the perfectionist strivings record so that your spiritual adviser has a written record of your goals and values. A verbal discussion will end up being too general and of little value in correcting faulty beliefs. Second, you must avoid asking for repeated reassurances from the spiritual guide on whether your religious goals, values, and practices are appropriate or not. Go over the perfectionist strivings record once with your spiritual guide and write down his or her evaluations of the record. It is important that you refrain from further discussion of the record, even if you have questions and doubts after the session. Repeated reassurance will only make your obsessions worse, and it will undermine your attempts to change your thinking.

FOCUS EXERCISE 9.4: COST/BENEFIT ANALYSIS

Another useful exercise for challenging your moral perfectionism beliefs is to conduct a cost/benefit analysis. Go back to Focus Exercise 9.3 and copy the first two columns of the perfectionist strivings record. This will give you one column with your moral/religious goals and values, as well as a second column with the ways you attempt to achieve these goals and values. In a third column, write down all the costs associated with striving to achieve this moral/religious goal, and in a fourth column, write down all the benefits derived from having this goal. The following is an example of Bob's cost/benefit analysis of his first moral goal, to be totally honest in his interactions with others.

Moral Goals/ Values	Ways to Achieve Moral Goals/Values	Costs of This Goal	Benefits of This Goal
1. Be totally honest in my inter- actions with others.	Repeat conversations to ensure complete honesty. Repeatedly question others to ensure I have not communicated a falsehood. Avoid social conversation to reduce the chances of spreading a falsehood.	Feel very upset after I talk to others. Distress while conversing so high that I can't concentrate on the conversation. Feel alone and isolated because I avoid social conversations. Friends and family get upset at me because I keep correcting myself. I feel like people think I'm weird because I repeat myself so much. I waste a lot of time correcting and repeating myself, so my work does not get done and I feel more stress. I've had several warnings at work because I am so slow.	I feel good for a little while if I feel certain that I've been completely honest. I feel good about myself when I know I've been completely honest. I am following Jesus' command to be honest, above reproach, in thought, word, and deed.

Go back over your cost/benefit sheet and for each moral/religious goal or value, rate how often you achieve this moral/religious perfection from 0 (never) to 10 (always). What would it take to improve your success rate at achieving the goal or value? What would be the additional costs? Would it be worth it? As it currently stands, do the benefits outweigh the costs of your moral perfectionism strivings? The purpose of this cost/benefit analysis is to challenge your belief that it is desirable, advantageous, and therefore necessary to pursue moral/ religious perfectionism.

If you conclude that your moral perfectionism beliefs are a significant contributor to your religious obsessions and compulsions, it is important to replace these beliefs with healthier goals and values.

These alternative beliefs should be a better reflection of the actual values of your faith community, and they should counter your obsessional concerns and fears.

FOCUS EXERCISE 9.5: ALTERNATIVE GOALS/VALUES

We suggest that you work out alternative moral and faith-based goals and values using this exercise. Redo Focus Exercise 9.4, by writing down alternative goals/values in the first column and rules that you will follow to fulfill these goals and values in the second column. The following is an alternative goals/value table that Bob worked out with his pastoral counselor and therapist to replace his perfectionistic striving for honesty.

Moral Goals/ Values	Ways to Achieve Moral Goals/Values	Level of Distress (0 to 100)	Level of Success (0 to 100)
1. To communicate self-perceived truth without willful deception to others.	To communicate my recollection of past events to others without qualifying myself (avoid phrases like "I'm not sure but . . . ," "Well, I think . . . ," "I might be wrong but . . ."). Avoid repeating phrases or retelling events, no matter how much doubt or distress I feel. Speak clearly and quickly in conversation and refrain from evaluating every word or phrase before I utter it. Refrain from asking others whether they understand what I just said. Remind myself that I have not engaged in willful deception, no matter how poor or inaccurate my recollection of events.		

Intolerance of Uncertainty

As discussed previously, excessive and debilitating doubt is very often at the heart of scrupulosity. In order to relieve the distress associated with this painful doubt, people with religious obsessions often strive to attain an absolute level of certainty in order to counter their doubts. Erica suffered from persistent obsessional doubts about whether she had committed the "unpardonable sin that grieved the Holy Spirit." She believed that God could not forgive such a sin, and so she would be condemned to eternal damnation. Erica's obsessions took the form of doubt; she was in a near constant state of worry over whether or not she had committed the "unpardonable sin." It was not that she believed she had committed sin, but rather, her obsession always took the form of the question, "Could I have committed the unpardonable sin?" To relieve her doubts, she compulsively prayed for forgiveness and sought reassurance from others about whether or not a certain thought or feeling might be an "unforgivable sin." Erica would repeat prayers over and over again until she felt certain that she had not committed the sin. The problem was that she hardly ever gained the level of certainty she sought. So the doubts, distress, and repeating compulsions continued unabated.

Gaining Perspective

To gain perspective, first consider whether it is possible to attain the level of certainty necessary to effectively vanquish your obsessional doubts. A second issue is whether the very act of trying to be certain "that you pleased God," "that you have not sinned," "that you are ritualistically clean or pure," or "that you sincerely confessed all your sins," in fact, can be counterproductive. Is it possible that the very act of trying to be certain is actually increasing your obsessional doubt and distress, rather than eliminating it?

FOCUS EXERCISE 9.6: CERTAINTY EVALUATION RECORD

This exercise helps you deal with faulty beliefs and appraisals about the need for certainty. The first step is to obtain information on the effects of intolerance of uncertainty on your obsessional doubts. Once every day for the next week, record the time your doubt occurred, your level of certainty, how long your sense of certainty lasted, the costs of pursuing certainty, and the benefits of trying to attain certainty. Below is an example of how Erica used this record to deal with her obsessive doubt, "Did I commit the unpardonable sin?"

Erica's obsessional doubt: "Did I commit the unpardonable sin which would lead to eternal damnation?"

Erica's certainty criteria: "I must feel the assurance of the Holy Spirit that I am right with God. This means that I will have no anxiety and no doubt about God's forgiveness of my wrongdoing."

Date/Time Obsession Occurred	Level of Certainty (0=none; 100= absolute)	Duration of Attained Certainty	Costs of Pursuing Certainty	Benefits of Attaining Certainty
Sept. 10, 2:35 p.m.	64	10 min.	Spent one hour on phone to pastor; got no work done. Could tell pastor was very frustrated with me. I was very upset, crying. The doubt seemed to grow the more I searched for assurance of forgiveness. Relative peace of mind lasted only a few minutes and then doubt returned.	I eventually did feel some assurance of forgiveness. Had about ten minutes of relative peace of mind. Learned a new Scripture verse.

Sept. 11, 8:45 p.m.	35	3 min.	Felt very hopeless and suicidal. Certainty of forgiveness was particularly elusive today.	Kept my mind off all the work that was piling up. Avoided housework.

After you have recorded a number of occurrences of your obses-sional doubt, go back over your chart. How often were you able to attain an acceptable level of certainty? How often did you fail to attain certainty, even after considerable effort? How long did the assurance of certainty last? Did the costs outweigh the benefits? Was there any evidence that your attempt to achieve certainty made the doubt stronger or more persistent?

Another approach for gaining perspective on your intolerance of uncertainty is to show your spiritual guide or pastoral counselor your completed certainty evaluation record. Discuss with your counselor whether it is possible or even desirable to achieve absolute certainty in all moral decisions and matters of faith. Show your counselor the lengths you have gone to achieve this absolute certainty. Ask your counselor whether she or he would survey five colleagues on how they are able to experience God's forgiveness in their own life. Do they experience doubt? If so, how do they deal with it? Your spiritual counselor should report back to you on the results of his/her mini-survey. It is also important that you discuss with your spiritual guide or pastoral counselor an alternative perspective on your religious doubts. Once this alternative belief has been developed, it is important that you write it down in your notebook and refer to it when doing the exposure exercise below.

The cornerstone of most religious devotion is faith, not certainty. In fact, the search for certainty may actually undermine faith. Thus, the alternative belief will probably incorporate some reminder of the importance of faith in personal religious experience. Erica developed the following alternative belief with the help of her pastoral counselor:

God is all loving and forgiving. He desires that all living human beings have a personal relationship with Him. Therefore the probability that a person will commit an unforgivable sin is exceedingly remote because this goes against God's forgiving nature. It is by faith, not by intellectual argument or certainty, that we have a relationship with God.

FOCUS EXERCISE 9.7: CHALLENGING THE NEED FOR CERTAINTY

Here are two behavioral experiments that will help you abandon your counterproductive attempts to achieve certainty. The first experiment involves a further investigation of the negative effects of intolerance of uncertainty. Choose a task that in the past has never been associated with doubt. Over the next week, repeatedly throughout the day bring up doubts about your action and then try to reassure yourself that you completed it perfectly or completely. Write down any observations about what happens to your feelings about this task.

For example, Erica selected brushing her teeth in the morning as the target behavior for this exercise. Erica had never had any obsessional doubts about whether she brushed her teeth in the morning. Over the next week, Erica frequently questioned herself throughout the day, "Did I really brush my teeth this morning?" "How do I know I brushed my teeth?" "Maybe I'm just imagining I brushed them." "Maybe I am getting my days mixed up." "Maybe I forgot to brush them this morning." "Maybe I didn't brush them well enough and there is still food lodged between my teeth that could cause a cavity." Erica also tried to counter these artificial doubts by searching for evidence that proved she had brushed her teeth. What she discovered from this exercise is that you can generate a doubt over any action, and this doubt can never be eliminated by searching for certain proof. In the end, the search for certainty only fueled the doubt.

Like all faulty appraisals and beliefs, the best treatment for intolerance of uncertainty is exposure. It is important to repeatedly practice generating the obsessional doubt and then to refrain from carrying out any response that involves a search for certainty or reassurance.

For Erica, this meant exposing herself to situations or stimuli that triggered her doubt, "Did I commit the unpardonable sin?" This involved at least three half-hour sessions daily in which Erica would sit and think about committing sin. Even though her anxiety level rose, Erica prevented herself from saying any prayers of confession or forgiveness. She also refrained from reciting Scripture verses or seeking reassurance from others about her sinfulness. Instead, she maintained a concentrated focus on the thought, "Did I commit the unpardonable sin?" Over time, Erica noticed that her level of distress during the exposure sessions became much less intense. It also became harder to sustain her attention to the unpardonable-sin thought. Her urge to seek certainty also became less intense. This led to a significant reduction in her doubts. Eventually, Erica was able to return to church and actively participate in the worship service without experiencing distracting doubts and an unrelenting search for assurance.

Control of Thoughts

The belief that you must exercise better, or even complete, control over your obsessions is a core appraisal or belief that is characteristic of most forms of obsessional thinking, not just scrupulosity. Individuals with OCD often believe that the reason they have obsessions is that they lack mental control. If only they had as much mental control as nonobsessional individuals, then they would be free of their OCD.

There are two problems with this belief. First, it assumes that mental control over unwanted distressing thoughts is possible, and second, it assumes that by trying harder to control your obsessions, your OCD symptoms will become less frequent and distressing. But what if the opposite were true? What if it is not possible to control obsessional thoughts, and, in fact, the more you try to control the thoughts, the worse your OCD?

Gaining Perspective

Chapter 7 dealt with the issue of the control of unwanted intrusive thoughts or obsessions. Review that chapter and, in particular, your results with the "white bear" experiment (Focus Exercise 7.1). How successful was your attempt to suppress white bear thoughts?

FOCUS EXERCISE 9.8: CONTROL AND RELIGIOUS OBSESSIONS

Do Focus Exercise 7.1 again, but this time substitute your primary religious obsession for the white bear thought. First, purposefully think about the obsession for two minutes and record each time your concentration drifts. Next, try to suppress or not think about the obsession for two minutes and record each time the obsession pops back into your mind. Write down your observations. Were you more successful at keeping your attention focused on the obsession than on thoughts of white bears? Why do you suppose it was easier to concentrate on the obsession than white bears? Is it because the obsession is a more significant or important thought? Now look at the success of suppressing the thought. Were you more successful at suppressing white bears than the religious obsession? Could it be that the obsession is more difficult to control because you've built this into a highly important and significant thought?

Another exercise that is useful for gaining perspective on your belief is to write out a brief explanation in your notebook about why it is important to control the obsession. After writing down your control script, conduct a mini-survey among a few valued friends or family members who share your faith. Find out their perspective on the control of religious doubt. How does their understanding of the control of religious doubt differ from yours?

Stephanie was a devout Roman Catholic who experienced extremely repugnant obsessive blasphemous thoughts and images of Jesus and Mary engaging in sex. These thoughts and images were most likely to occur while taking Holy Communion, praying, or whenever she was reminded of her faith. Stephanie believed that it was very important to banish these thoughts and images from her mind. If the thoughts were allowed to linger, she would feel dirty, and her anxiety would escalate to the point where it was unbearable. She was afraid that the blasphemous thoughts would eventually lead to a nervous breakdown that would result in a long hospitalization. She feared the breakdown would leave enduring emotional scars that could result in an inability to return to work and the loss of her family. Indeed, Stephanie felt that everything, her very life, hinged on gaining control over the blasphemous obsessions.

When Stephanie wrote her control script and conducted her mini-survey, she was surprised to find that other people also experience the occasional unwanted, even naughty, thought or image while in church. Although the thoughts were not as repugnant as Stephanie's obsessions, nevertheless, they were unwanted and somewhat distressing to people. Moreover, Stephanie discovered that people did not share her belief that these thoughts had to be controlled or dire consequences would occur. Instead, they would say a single brief prayer and then "leave it with God." That is, they did not actively try to suppress the thought, but instead let it "float" out of their minds more naturally. Stephanie's fellow believers told her that they do not believe that unwanted thoughts are a threat to your faith. They believed that thoughts that enter the mind against your will are not sinful and so they do not try to control them. They treat these thoughts as if they were not their own thoughts but rather the ideas of a stranger.

The alternative to controlling a thought is ignoring it, or letting go of the obsession. Based on your own experience with mental control, you can turn the paradox of control to your own advantage. Letting the obsession fade on its own will eventually lead to a reduction in the obsession and its associated distress. Letting go of the obsession will be very hard at first. Your natural tendency will be to try to control it, suppress it, or dismiss it. The only way you will be able to refrain from your habitual mental control efforts and compulsions is to adopt an alternative approach to mental control. The alternative interpretation is this: "The less I control the obsession, the more quickly it will spontaneously fade."

> "The less I control the obsession, the more quickly it will spontaneously fade."

FOCUS EXERCISE 9.9: ALTERNATE CONTROL

Once again, exposure and behavioral experimentation are critical to learning how to relinquish control over your obsession. There are a number of "countercontrol" behavioral exercises described by Clark (2004), Rachman (2003), and Morrison and Westbrook (2004) that you can use in this regard. For example, begin by experimenting with "no control" experiences or days versus "control" days. Record in your notebook the effects of "control" versus "no control" days. Stephanie, for example, compared the effects of going to church and actively trying to push blasphemous thoughts and images from her mind versus going to church and letting the thoughts/images fade from her mind without active control. The following is a sample of her alternate control record.

Type of Experience	Control Response	Level of Distress (0 to 100)	Percentage of Time Spent with Blasphemous Thought
"control" church service	Repeatedly said prayers of confession. Kept repeating the phrase "Holy Mary Mother of God, I beseech thee." Tried to replace blasphemous image with image of the crucified Christ.	90	Had blasphemous thoughts/images during 65 percent of the service
"no control" church service	Did nothing; let the thoughts/images come and go on their own.	At first 95 percent distress, but by end of service fell to 50 percent.	At first the obsessions were constant, but by end of service I was able to think of other things (60 percent).

no control service	Did nothing.	Overall distress was 40 percent.	Only 25 percent of time spent on obsession.

Stephanie learned from her alternative control record that the best way to deal with her OCD symptoms was to refrain from trying to control her blasphemous thoughts and images. Eventually, over time, her obsessions and mental compulsions declined to practically nothing. Although she continues to view the blasphemous thoughts and images as repugnant, she has learned that the best way to counter the obsession is to let it fade naturally, on its own, and to refrain from any compulsion or other response designed to control it.

In order to quicken your treatment response, it's important to move from alternative days of no control to regularly refraining from any efforts to control your obsession through compulsions, neutralization, or intentional mental control. The most effective approach to reducing religious obsessions and compulsions is to design your own exposure and response prevention sessions. This can be done by developing and implementing an exposure ladder as described in the next chapter. However, before turning to chapter 10, there is one final issue to mention concerning treatment of scrupulosity.

RELIGIOUS COUNSELING AND OCD TREATMENT

Throughout this chapter, we have emphasized the importance of receiving both psychological treatment and spiritual or pastoral counseling in the treatment of religious obsessions and compulsions. However, we recognize that it can be difficult to find the right combination of psychological treatment and spiritual counseling that will maximize the chances of treatment success.

There are three characteristics to look for when choosing a therapist to treat scrupulosity. First, the therapist should have a good working knowledge of OCD. Obsessions and compulsions are difficult to treat and can be made worse at the hands of a naïve or inexperienced therapist. Second, the therapist should have some training in CBT for anxiety disorders, and preferably OCD. There are numerous types of psychological theories and therapies, and so many psychologists are not familiar with the treatment approach described in this book. And third, the therapist should be respectful and comfortable treating religious obsessions and compulsions. It is not necessary for the therapist to be religious to treat scrupulosity, since scrupulosity is an aspect of OCD. However, the therapist must be respectful of your faith and be able to distinguish between faith practice and symptoms of OCD.

It may be even harder to find a spiritual guide or pastoral counselor from your faith community who can help you with your OCD. It's essential that any pastoral counseling you do receive is consistent with your psychological treatment. If not, you will be faced with opposing advice and contradictions that will only make your distress worse. A spiritual counselor should have some familiarity with OCD and should have experience working with mental-health professionals. In addition, it's important that your spiritual guide has high credibility in your eyes as someone who knows the details of your religious faith and doctrine. Above all, you should have some assurance from both your therapist and spiritual counselor that they can and will work together to offer you the best possible treatment for your scrupulosity.

TAKING THE PLUNGE: EXPOSURE

By gradually phasing out your compulsions, neutralizing, and avoidance, the goal of this chapter was to help you prepare to take acceptable risks. You may now be fully able and willing to take educated, calculated risks and be ready to plunge into exposure; if so, go for it!

> You have to put the information to the test by actually taking the risks. The longer you avoid doing exposure, the longer you will have your OCD.

Even if you still doubt that such risks are educated and calculated, we highly recommend that you begin exposure now; sometimes, you can talk about something over and over again, and it doesn't hit home, but taking the plunge does. You may be the kind of person who needs the experience of taking risks before your appraisal of your obsessions changes. Finally, you may be starting to use this new information as a form of compulsion or neutralizing; that is, when you get the obsession, you may review the information as a means of reducing your anxiety and find that you feel better for a while. This will not help you in the long run and, in fact, may make your OCD worse. You have to put the information to the test by actually taking the risks. The longer you avoid doing exposure, the longer you will have your OCD.

CHAPTER 10

Taking the Risk: Phasing Out Coping Strategies

RATIONALE FOR PHASING OUT COPING STRATEGIES

Throughout this book, we have emphasized the importance of challenging your assumptions about the meaning of your obsessions. The most powerful means of challenging your assumptions is to expose yourself to them while refraining from using compulsions, neutralizing, avoidance, and thought control. Recall that obsessional thoughts make you feel distress or discomfort of some kind, and compulsions and neutralizing are ways of reducing this distress or, at the very least, keeping it from becoming worse. This is a quick fix. Coping strategies can offer escape, avoidance, or immediate relief, but in the long term, by not allowing you to learn anything new about your obsessions and their true meaning, and by ensuring that you never have the opportunity to realize that the distress will go away on its own, they keep your OCD alive. When you repeatedly allow yourself to experience the obsession without using any of your coping strategies, you will have the opportunity to learn that the obsessional thought is actually a thought that you can safely ignore.

In exposure, you will allow yourself to have the obsession without using any of your coping strategies. Your distress over the obsession will eventually go down, even if you don't use your coping strategies, and in the absence of this distress, you will be in a much better position to evaluate, or appraise, the true meaning of the obsession. The more often you allow yourself to experience your obsession in the absence of coping strategies, the lower your emotional response to it will be, the faster it will decline, and the more balanced your appraisal of its meaning will be.

TAKING IT ONE STEP AT A TIME: THE EXPOSURE LADDER

Obsessions can cause varying levels of distress, depending upon a number of factors, but often according to where and when the obsession occurs and how you are feeling when it occurs. Exposure therapy begins with the development of a very specific list of situations that represent increasingly more and more difficult encounters with your obsessions. We call this an *exposure ladder*, because you begin with exposure to the situations at the bottom of the ladder, which cause you moderate distress, and work your way up the ladder until the top, where you expose yourself to the situations that cause you the most distress. At each step of the ladder, you will do exercises that actively evoke your obsession, and *you will refrain from using any of your coping strategies*. You will focus on the obsession and will continue the exercise until your distress decreases noticeably. You will then do the exercise again and again, until it no longer evokes much distress. Then you will move on to the next step in the ladder.

If your obsession is an impulse (say, of swerving into the next lane while driving or pushing someone in front of a subway train), you will expose yourself to the situation that evokes the impulse (driving on a busy street or standing on a subway platform). If your obsession is an image (a horrific image of harming a loved one, for example), you will expose yourself to that image by concentrating on it mentally, by writing it down in detail, or by exposing yourself to objects or situations that evoke it. If your obsession is a doubt ("What if I am gay?" "Am I a pedophile?"), you will expose yourself to the sense of doubt without engaging it in any way (by not seeking information consistent or inconsistent with the proposition you are doubting or by not monitoring your body for signs of sexual arousal in the presence of certain types of people); that is, you will behave as if the doubt is meaningless (even though you feel differently).

This chapter will help you develop a plan for stopping compulsions and neutralizing that is gradual and manageable, yet still highly effective. Some people are able to quit using all of their coping strategies cold turkey. If you are such a person, then you can skip to the last section of this chapter. If you do not think you can give up all your coping strategies at once, please read on.

IS IT DANGEROUS TO EXPERIENCE THIS LEVEL OF DISTRESS?

It is true that chronic, pervasive stress can lead to health problems, but the distress you will experience when you expose yourself to your obsession is unlike the ongoing, unrelenting stress over years that is associated with health problems. The toll on your body from the anxiety created during exposure has been likened to that of climbing up a flight of stairs. The distress you experience usually starts to reduce within thirty minutes or so, and it is certainly rare for the distress to last more than an hour without reducing in intensity. Some people are concerned that if they don't do their ritual when they have an obsession, it will bother them for the rest of the day, preventing them from being able to concentrate on other things. Again, it is unlikely that the feeling will last for a prolonged period of

> Use of the quick fix in response to your obsession means short-term gain for long-term pain. Exposure to your obsession without the quick fix means short-term pain for long-term gain.

time with an intensity that is disruptive to normal functioning. People typically find that distress is very high at first and takes a while to go down. However, after a few sessions of exposure, the distress goes up less high and tends to come down more quickly, and eventually the obsession results in very little distress and, therefore, very little perceived need to use a coping strategy. Use of the quick fix in response to your obsession means short-term gain for long-term pain. Exposure to your obsession without the quick fix means short-term pain for long-term gain.

FOCUS EXERCISE 10.1: BUILDING YOUR LADDER

To build your exposure ladder, we use a distress scale ranging from 0 (no distress at all) to 100 (the most distress an obsession can cause you). The ten-step ladder consists of ten situations involving experiencing your obsession without using any neutralizing, compulsions, thought control, escape, or avoidance. The situations increase in intensity from 1 to 10. To illustrate, here is the ladder Daphne constructed. Note that each exercise is listed assuming she cannot use her neutralizing, compulsions, thought control, escape, or avoidance.

Exercise	Distress
10. Having my obsession that I may have caused harm to elderly people by not being hygienic enough when I am volunteering on the night shift in a nursing home	100
9. Having my obsession of tripping people while I am volunteering in a nursing home	90
8. Having my obsession of tripping people when I am on the subway platform	85
7. Having my obsession of tripping people when I am walking on a busy street where there are lots of potential victims	80

6.	Having my obsession that I may have caused harm when I am with my family	70
5.	Having my obsession of tripping people when I am out on my own and am around young, healthy people	60
4.	Having my obsession that I may have caused harm when I am walking to class and I know the janitors are there to oversee things (mop up spills I may have made)	50
3.	Having my obsession of tripping people when I am with friends	50
2.	Having my obsession that I may have caused harm, but harm would most likely come to me than to someone else	40
1.	Having my obsession that I may have caused harm, but the harm is minor	30

Note several things about Daphne's ladder. First, the intensity of her obsession varies according to how vulnerable the potential "victims" are, how easy it would be to act on them (she feels she has more self-control when she is out with friends than when alone), and whether there are others around who could intervene to prevent harm should she have caused it (when she knows the janitors are there and can mop up spills). This is reflected by the placement of different situations on the ladder. When you construct your ladder, you will want to consider all of the factors that make your obsession easier or harder to tolerate. Second, all of these situations are situations that Daphne can easily put herself in on a regular basis. This is an important aspect of planning your hierarchy; all the situations on it must be ones you can put yourself in at least several times a week. Third, you will notice that Daphne began with a situation that causes moderate, as opposed to minimal, distress. This is because exercises that cause minimal distress are so easy that you do not get to experience a really noticeable drop in your distress level. If you were afraid of dogs, and you began your exposure with an exercise that causes only minimal distress (looking at a picture of a small, fluffy, friendly looking dog), you would not have the opportunity to learn that your emotional response to dogs is exaggerated, because you are not experiencing an exaggerated level of distress; that is, your distress does not drop enough in response to the exercise to realize that it was needlessly high in the first place. Furthermore, if you don't start a bit higher, it could take a very long time to work up the ladder.

Here is Juan's ladder. Juan was plagued by images of harming his grandchildren with a knife and organized his life around avoiding anything and anyone triggering these horrific images, such as the color red, any kind of violence on television, all sharp objects, and, of course, his grandchildren. He was terrified of the images themselves and instantly suppressed them the moment they occurred.

Exercise	Distress
10. Chopping vegetables while my grandchildren are with me in the kitchen	100
9. Holding a knife or other sharp object when my grandchildren are in the next room	90
8. Watching/reading anything with violence	85
7. Having the image when my grandchildren are around	80
6. Having the image while looking at a picture of my grandchildren	70
5. Holding a knife or other sharp object when my grandchildren are not around	65
4. Describing the image out loud	60
3. Wearing red	50
2. Talking about my grandchildren	45
1. Driving my son's red car	40

Here is Anke's ladder. Remember, all of these exercises assume no use of any coping strategies, such as seeking reassurance from her pastor or using ritualistic prayer.

Exercise	Distress
10. Doing a Bible reading during a church service	100
9. Having my worst blasphemous thought while in church praying for atonement and not doing anything about it	90
8. Having my worst blasphemous thought while reading my Bible and not doing anything about it	85
7. Reading a description of my worst blasphemous image aloud	80
6. Writing a description of my worst blasphemous image down on paper	75
5. Having my lesser blasphemous image in church and not doing anything about it	70
4. Attending a Bible study group	60
3. Having my blasphemous images while volunteering at the soup kitchen	50
2. Cutting out my hourly prayers	45
1. Having my lesser blasphemous image at home and not doing anything about it	40

Instructions: To begin your ladder, first identify the various obsessions you have. If you have obsessions that tend to be unrelated to each other (such as an obsession of swerving into the next lane while driving and an obsession as to whether or not you have offended God), you will want to build separate ladders for each. Now make a chart just like the sample charts above, with ten rows, numbered from ten down to one, and two columns. Label the left-hand column "exercise" and the right-hand column "distress," as in the sample ladders. Now review your obsessions, neutralizing, and compulsions (you may wish to refer to Focus Exercises 4.1 and 4.2 in your notebook). Think about how much distress it would cause you to focus on each of your obsessions *without using each of your coping strategies; that is, no compulsions, neutralizing, thought control, escape, or avoidance.* Now think about the factors that make your obsession more or less intense and your neutralizing/compulsion feel more or less necessary.

At the top of the chart, on line ten, write in the event that would be the most distressing in the left-hand column (90 to 100 on the distress scale) and write in the associated distress level in the right-hand column. Now go to the bottom of the chart, on line one, and write in an event that would be only moderately distressing in the left-hand column (would be 30 to 40 on the distress scale) and the distress level in the right-hand column. Go to line six on your chart and write in the event that would be higher in distress but not the highest (would be about 60 to 70 on the distress scale). Using the same principle, fill in the other lines.

You can vary the factors that affect your distress over the obsession and/or the strength of your urge to complete the neutralizing act or compulsion. See the following section for some specific suggestions for doing exposure exercises. Keep in mind that your ladder is not written in stone, so don't worry if you're not certain about the exact amount of distress a situation will cause you. You can move steps around, as necessary, later on; instead, build the ladder based on your best guess.

DOING EXPOSURE EXERCISES

Now that you have a good working exposure ladder, it's time to begin exposure. In exposure, you tackle each situation on your ladder in order, beginning with the first and ending with the tenth. For example, Daphne would start by allowing herself to have her obsession about causing minor harm and would not use her normal coping strategies. In order to do this, she would plan to deliberately put herself in situations that would evoke the obsession, such as shopping in a busy mall or walking on a busy street. As she experiences her obsession regarding minor harm, she will focus on that obsession but refrain from using any of her coping strategies. She will stay in the situation until her distress declines. Then she will put herself back in that situation as soon as possible, and again allow herself to experience the obsession without using any coping strategies. She will do this as often as possible. If Daphne experiences that particular obsession outside of her planned exposure sessions, she will still refrain from using her coping strategies. When Daphne's distress over the obsession of causing minor harm becomes negligible, she will be ready to move on to the next step of her ladder.

Juan would begin by driving his son's car as often as possible. If he has his obsession while driving, he will refrain from using any of his usual coping strategies. When driving the car causes negligible distress, he will be ready to move on to the next step on his ladder. You should proceed similarly with the steps in your ladder. There are three basic rules to exposure:

1. Do not use *any* of your coping strategies in response to the obsession during exposure nor afterwards (don't simply postpone use of coping strategies until after the exposure session is over).

2. Stay in the situation until your distress decreases noticeably.

3. Repeat the exercise again as soon as possible.

KEYS TO SUCCESSFUL EXPOSURE

Here are some suggestions for making steady progress.

Make It Planned, Repeated, Frequent

Decide how, when, and where you are going to do the exercise to make sure you plan time often enough in the week to benefit from it. The more often you do it, the better off you are. We know from research that doing one exposure daily for ten days is far more effective in reducing distress in the long term than doing one exposure weekly for ten weeks. Sometimes people give up after a few tries at exposure if their distress stays high for a long time. Remember, the more often you do it, the lower your distress will be initially, and the faster it will decline. We have yet to work with anyone whose distress did not decline when exposure was conducted properly. You need to stick with it. It is much like starting a program of physical exercise. At first the exercises are hard, and the benefits are few. The more you do it, though, the easier it gets and the more benefits you start to enjoy.

Expect to Feel Distress

Expect to feel distress when you do the exposure. That's the whole point! If you don't actually feel the distress, you will not gain any benefits from doing the exercise. Dr. Martin Antony, a world-recognized expert in treatment of anxiety and OCD, counsels people to accept the distress and not fight it (Antony and Swinson 2000). He also counsels people to judge their success according to what they did during the exercise, not how they felt. Remember, short-term pain for long-term gain!

Take It into Your "Real" Life

The rules of exposure apply to your planned exposure sessions, as well as to times when you are faced with the situation spontaneously, in your real life. If you limit refraining from using your coping strategies to your exposure sessions, you will be making things harder for yourself; if you are refraining from coping strategies during some instances (during deliberate exposure) but not others (when the obsession occurs outside of deliberate exposure), you will teach yourself that when you refrain from your coping strategies, you feel distress, but when you use them you feel way better. This, of course, makes it significantly harder to refrain the next time.

Resist the Urge!

Dr. Gail Steketee, a world-renowned expert in treatment of OCD, advises that you must resist the urge to use all coping strategies connected to current and previous exposure exercises (Steketee 1999). Expect to be very tempted to use your quick fix coping strategy to bring down your distress. This is normal, but you must not give in to the urge, especially when your distress is high and the urge is strong. If you use your coping strategies while your distress is high, you will feel exceptional relief, and it will be that much more difficult to resist the urge to use them the next time. If you give in to the urge, do the exercise again, as soon as you can.

Sometimes people get through an exposure exercise by promising themselves that they will do their neutralizing act or compulsion later. This defeats the purpose of the exposure; first, you should not be attempting to decrease your distress during the exposure. Second, the purpose of exposure is to help you learn that your coping strategies are ultimately unnecessary, and the effort you put into doing the exercise will be nullified when you perform the act.

Pace Yourself Up the Ladder

Go at your own pace. If you are able to extinguish your distress over the first situation within a few days, by all means, move on to the

If you use your coping strategies while your distress is high, you will feel exceptional relief, and it will be that much more difficult to resist the urge to use them the next time.

next step. If it takes a week of regular exposure for distress to decline, then take that week. If it is taking more than a week, then the step may be too high, and you may want to adjust the situation by altering the circumstances under which you expose yourself. Sometimes you may err in your prediction about how distressing a particular exposure exercise will be. Sometimes people find that the situation causes considerably more or considerably less distress than they anticipated. When this happens, you can simply move the situation to its appropriate spot on the ladder and work on the steps you can manage.

What should you do when faced with situations in real life that are higher on the ladder than the one you are working on? Dr. Steketee (1999) suggests that you can use coping strategies for exposure situations higher on the ladder than where you are currently working; however, she strongly recommends that if you do use a coping strategy, you expose yourself again to your most recently practiced items on the hierarchy, so you also get practice at refraining from the use of coping strategies.

Continue Exposure

When you advance a step, you must continue to expose yourself to all the situations on the previous steps! If after successfully completing steps five and six on the ladder, Juan starts avoiding driving his son's car again, talking about his grandchildren, and describing his image out loud, his distress over the obsession and his urge to use other coping strategies will escalate again. This is because he has only had a few recent experiences without finding these situations stressful, compared to many experiences of being afraid of them. The same goes for your obsessions; you will want your experiences of having the obsession without distress to outweigh your experiences of having the obsession with distress.

Reward Yourself

Exposure requires courage and hard work. To acknowledge this, you may want to reward yourself every week for doing successful exposure. You can promise yourself a new CD, or dinner out, or a luxurious bath, whatever is rewarding for you.

Here's a quick summary of the keys to success:

Guidelines for Exposure

1. Plan repeated, regular exposure exercises frequently throughout the week; reserve time in your day planner to ensure you protect time to do them.

2. Expect to experience distress.

3. Don't try to fight the distress; let it wash over you.

4. Expect to have strong urges to use your coping strategies, but don't give in to those urges! If you do, try again as soon as possible or scale the exercise back to something more manageable.

5. Do your exposure exercises as often as you can, as close in time as you can.

6. Don't be discouraged if your distress takes a long time to come down at first; keep trying.

7. Judge the success of the exercise by what you did, not by how you felt during it.

8. Pace yourself so that you are consistently challenged but not so overwhelmed that you are unable to resist using coping strategies.

9. Continue doing the exercises in steps you have already conquered.

10. Reward yourself weekly for successful exposure.

FOCUS EXERCISE 10.2:
DOING EXPOSURE EXERCISES

In your notebook, record when, where, and how you are going to do the first step in your ladder. You may want to actually schedule these exercises into your daybook so that you protect your time to do them. Plan for at least four exposures per week, and more if possible. In the beginning, reread the keys to successful exposure above before starting an exposure, until you really know what to expect and what to do. It is important to recognize that exposure can be tiring, and you may want to cut back on some of your voluntary activities for the first week or two that you are doing it. You may be more irritable than usual, as well. Keep in mind that it won't always be like this; exposure will become less and less of an effort the more you do it.

Now, let's go! Before and after each exposure session record the following:

■   date and time

■   situation

■   distress level (0 to 100)

During exposure:

■   Remain focused on the obsession and allow yourself to experience the distress (do not distract yourself from the situation in any way).

■   Use statements such as "this is difficult but if I stick it out it will pay off" or "this distress is unpleasant but it is not dangerous," and "I can do this" (*do not* attempt to trivialize, minimize, or distract yourself from the threat the obsession actually represents to you).

■   Stay focused in the present, rather than on what is going to happen next (do not catastrophize about the consequences of exposure).

If you give in and use your coping strategies, try again as soon as possible. If you give in again, then modify the exercise, so it is more manageable. Review chapters 8 or 9 to help bolster your confidence that it is safe to have your obsession without using a coping strategy.

At the end of the first week, plot your distress level over time on a graph, like the one presented in Focus Exercise 5.1. Graph the distress levels from the first exposure session. Using a different color, graph the distress levels from the second exposure episode, and so on. What you are likely to find is that in the beginning, your distress was very high and came down slowly, but that by the end, the distress was much lower and came down more quickly.

HOW TOS OF EXPOSURE

There are many situations people can encounter when they do exposure. This section describes typical situations and what to do about them.

When to Move Up the Ladder

When your distress over a situation is fairly low (20 to 25 on the distress scale) over several occurrences, it is time to move up to the next step on the ladder. Once again, plan when, where, and how you will do the exposure, and plan to do at least four exposures per week. Continue this until you have conquered the top step of your ladder. Keep in mind, though, that you need to continue exposing yourself to every item in the ladder.

What If Your Obsession Occurs Constantly?

Sometimes obsessions, especially those in the form of doubts, can be almost constant. The key to overcoming these is simply perseverance; you must expose yourself to the obsession and use no coping strategy each and every time it occurs. We have both worked with people who had constant doubts of one kind or another. They had to constantly allow themselves to experience the doubt without engaging it in any way; that is, they experienced the feeling of doubt without doing anything to make it better, such as checking or seeking reassurance. This was quite difficult for the first couple of weeks, but in each case, persistence began to pay off, and the doubts began to become far less intense and frequent.

If You Have More Than One Ladder

You may have a couple of ladders, reflecting different obsessional thoughts. We suggest working through both ladders at the same time, doing exercises of about the same intensity from each one.

When Compulsions and Neutralizing Are Excessive Forms of Important and Necessary Actions

During exposure, you will need to refrain from using any of your coping strategies, with the eventual goal of eliminating all use of them. However, some coping strategies are normal or necessary actions (washing your hands, praying, checking on the safety of your children). They are only compulsive and problematic when they are driven by obsessional fears ("Maybe I stabbed my child when I hugged her, but didn't know it"), as opposed to rationally determined criteria ("My child was playing in the backyard, but I don't hear her anymore"), and are repeated excessively (see chapter 2). For example, some people with OCD wash their hands several times an hour. Yet, handwashing is an activity necessary for maintaining appropriate standards of hygiene. Daphne was training to be a nurse and had thoughts that she might have harmed someone by not being careful enough. When dispensing medication, she would check and recheck the medication type and dosage before administering it. After administering it, she would immediately be concerned that she had erred and return to check the bottle and the patient's chart for dosage. Daphne was unable to complete her dispensing duties within the necessary time frame and often had to seek help from others. All health-care professionals need to be quite careful and conscientious in their practice, but Daphne's level of checking actually interfered with her ability to provide adequate care.

Anke's strong religious beliefs are an important part of her life and her identity. She used prayer to manage blasphemous thoughts and images. As an observant Christian, it is extremely important that Anke pray, but Anke's frequency of prayer and the distress she experienced during it actually interfered with her relationship with God. Of course, we would not want Anke to stop praying altogether, because it is a key form of her religious expression. Here's another example. Kenjiro's four-year-old son had a peanut allergy, and Kenjiro was so preoccupied with protecting his son from contact with nuts that he barely permitted him to leave the house. Obviously, some precautions against contact with nuts are necessary, but Kenjiro's precautions were so excessive that they actually interfered with his son's social and emotional development.

So, how do you strike an appropriate balance? We advise people to first identify an authority on matters relevant to the obsession and consult him or her *just once* to establish appropriate guidelines for behavior. In Daphne's case, we would ask her to apprise herself of the precautionary standards recommended by either the training program or the health-care centers in which she works, and limit her precautions to those. In Anke's case, we would ask her to consult her pastor *once* for advice on how frequently and under what circumstances to pray, and to pray only according to those guidelines. We would ask Kenjiro to consult an allergist about appropriate lengths to take for preventing his son from coming into contact with peanuts and to limit his precautions to those.

You may find that you have to accept some level of ambiguity, and rely on your own judgment, rather than be certain if performing an action is appropriate or not. A second rule of thumb to use is this: if it feels like OCD, it is! That is, if you feel that your desire to engage in a particular action is being driven by OCD rather than by an appropriate guideline, then it probably is, and you should refrain from engaging in the act.

TROUBLESHOOTING

This section identifies common problems in exposure and how to overcome them.

Your Distress Was Too Low

If your distress isn't high, it could mean that the step in the ladder is too low (that is, the situation simply doesn't cause a whole lot of distress to begin with). When you build your exposure ladder, you can't always predict what your distress will be, and you may find that situations you thought would be really frightening are actually not too bad. If this is the case, then simply move ahead a step.

If your distress is too low, though, it could mean instead that you are using some coping strategies to manage your distress during exposure. You need to examine what happened during exposure. Were you, in fact, using some strategies to manage your distress, such as distraction (when Juan first tried driving his son's car, he listened to loud music in order to avoid having his obsessions), or self-reassurance (when Daphne was walking down the street having her obsession of causing minor harm, she repeatedly told herself, "It's only two more blocks—only two more blocks and I am done, and as soon as I am done with this exercise, I am going to do my compulsion!"), or actual use of a compulsion or neutralizing act? One sign that you're using neutralizing or compulsions is if your distress goes up at first but comes down really rapidly.

Your Distress Was Too High

Again, you can't always predict how much distress a situation might cause. If your distress is overwhelming, and you are unable to resist using a coping strategy, you may need to either move back a step altogether, or modify the exercise to make it less distressing.

Your Distress Didn't Decrease

If you repeatedly focus on your obsession for a very long time, and your distress does not decrease, it could mean that the step is too high, and you need to go back a step. It could also mean that you are using some kind of neutralizing act or compulsion. We know from research that checking rituals can be associated with sustained, or even escalating, distress. For example, if you are spending time in your exposure rationalizing the thought (such as proving to yourself that it won't happen or that you are not a pedophile or murderer), your distress is unlikely to decrease. It is also possible that you are avoiding certain aspects of the situation, such as avoiding focusing on the act represented in the thought (focusing on the words "kill my grandchildren" rather than the actual image that is the obsession), so your response to the obsession cannot extinguish. You need to be sure that you are spending your exposure time focused on the obsession without using a single coping strategy. Finally, you want to make sure that you refrain from focusing on the consequences of not using your coping strategies; instead, simply focus on the obsession at hand. That is, keep focused in the present moment and deal with the aftermath later.

Exposure Ruins Your Day

You may find that after exposure you experience an especially persistent recurrence of the thought. This is also not a reason to discontinue exposure. You will need to continue refraining from your coping strategies. Keep in mind that as you do repeated exposure, you will become less bothered, rather than more bothered, by the thought; again, persistence is the key. You may also find that you are reluctant to do exposure on bad days, because you feel more fragile, or on good days, when you want to enjoy yourself a bit. What we tell people is that if you are having a bad day, then what does it matter to make it a bit worse by doing exposure as well? Furthermore, the impact of exposure on a bad day, when your mood is low, can actually be quite powerful; if you can become less distressed by your thought when you are feeling especially bad, you have had a powerful, valuable new learning experience, and exposure on regular or good days will seem easier by comparison. Exposure on a good day can also be really powerful in that you may be able to conquer more and have the opportunity to enjoy your success.

Your Symptoms of Anxiety Overwhelm You

Some people find their obsessions problematic because they trigger an anxiety response that they find intolerable. For example, when his obsession of harming children occurred, Kong Lee would experience heart racing, dizziness, shortness of breath, and nausea. He would then become extremely concerned that he might be having a heart attack. Kong Lee found the idea of exposure really difficult to accept because his anxiety response was so dramatic and upsetting. Here are several strategies for overcoming this problem. First, it is important for you to know and remember that the symptoms of anxiety are created by the activation of the fight-or-flight response, which is a very ancient response we all have that originally allowed us to survive as a species. When the fight-or-flight response is activated, the brain prepares the body to survive what it perceives as mortal danger. Blood flow is redirected to the large muscle groups, away from the extremities. This can lead to tingling sensations in the hands and feet. Your heart rate increases in order to increase blood flow to the muscles. This increase can be quite dramatic and feel as if you are having a heart attack. Your breathing increases in order to oxygenate the blood. However, sometimes shallow breathing occurs, which leads to faintness and dizziness, as well as choking and suffocating sensations. Digestion may speed up or slow down. All of these responses are natural and not dangerous. Your brain will eventually "turn off" this response, as well. Thus, the changes will not continue to accelerate. It is possible that many symptoms you thought of as fairly diverse, or as indicative of a heart attack, are in fact normal symptoms of anxiety.

A second strategy for overcoming concern about physical sensations is to actually expose yourself to the sensations you fear, using exactly the same procedures as outlined for exposure to your obsessions. For example, if you fear increases in heart rate, then deliberately do things to increase your heart rate (jogging or marching on the spot or running up stairs) and allow yourself to tolerate the sensations. If you are afraid of fast breathing, try breathing through a straw by plugging your nose, inserting the straw in your mouth, and breathing through it. If you don't like dizziness, then spin yourself in a chair and tolerate the sensations. You will quickly get used to the sensations, and they will begin to bother you much less.

EXPOSURE EXERCISES AND YOUR FAMILY

Dr. Steketee has worked extensively with individuals who have OCD and their families. She advises that family members can help if they are supportive and encouraging of effort and gains, as opposed to critical of setbacks or of the rate of progress (Steketee 1999). She also suggests that family members can help by assisting in generating ideas for exposure and for refraining from rituals.

Family members of people with OCD often want to help, but don't know how. Family members find it very upsetting to watch their loved one experience distress and often do what they can to alleviate that distress, such as offering repeated reassurance, assisting the individual in avoiding situations that trigger the obsession, tolerating compulsions and neutralizing acts, and agreeing to follow the person's "rules." In the short term, this serves to reduce the family member's distress, but in the long term, this accommodation of the obsession serves the same function as compulsions and neutralizing. If others tend to come to your aid when you are having your obsession, you will need to ask them to refrain from helping you.

If you tend to involve family or friends in reducing your distress over obsessions, it will be important for them to stop providing you with this assistance. You might want to give them this book to read, or, at the very least, this chapter and some of the earlier ones. They will be better able to withstand your short term distress if they understand that assisting you in reducing your distress in the short term is actually causing you more distress in the long run. You will then want to work out with them a kind and respectful way they can decline to participate in your coping strategies. In turn, when your obsessions are intense and you are desperate for relief, you need to plan to be respectful of them when they decline assistance. Here are some guidelines for helping family members refrain from "rescuing" you when you are distressed over your obsessions:

- Ensure that they understand the purpose and importance of exposure to your recovery from OCD (invite them read this book, or at least this chapter and a couple of the earlier chapters).

- Establish in advance what they should say to you if you do ask for assistance or otherwise involve them in your avoidance or in reducing your distress. Here are some examples: "We agreed that I am not to do this for you, because if I do, it will help your OCD, not you." Or, "I am committed to our agreement that I not help you with this so that you can get better."

- Emotions can get high when obsessions are intense, but resist the urge to lash out at someone because they are denying you assistance.

- Acknowledge the person's effort; just as it is easier in the moment for you to give in to your coping strategies, so it is much easier for him or her to give in to your requests for assistance.

- Family members are most helpful when they can take a nonjudgmental, supportive approach; mocking or trivializing your fears has no function in your recovery.

- Family members can offer support by reminding you of your gains, praising your efforts, and reminding you that hanging in there during an exposure will pay off for you.

QUITTING COLD TURKEY

Some people are able to give up using all of their coping strategies, cold turkey. There is no harm in doing this. Indeed, some of the most successful OCD treatment programs in the world advise it. The key to quitting, cold turkey, is actually quitting; that is, not sneaking in a subtle coping strategy or some avoidance in order to reduce distress, and being consistent in refraining from rituals, each and every time. People who quit smoking, cold turkey, do not allow themselves any cigarettes at all. If you decide to quit this way, be sure you have a thorough inventory of all of the strategies you use to manage your obsessions and that you are prepared to give them up. Expect to feel distress, and be prepared to endure it, keeping in mind that it is unpleasant but not dangerous. You need to avoid giving in and using a coping strategy, especially when your distress level is really high, because the relief will be enormous and it will be that much more difficult to resist using the strategy the next time.

CHAPTER 11

Maintaining Your Gains

REVIEWING YOUR GAINS

Success in overcoming OCD is best judged by your response to obsessional thoughts when you have them, not by the absence of obsessional thoughts. Recall that most people report having obsessional thoughts from time to time. What differentiates people without OCD from people with OCD is that people without OCD do not overinterpret the meaning of their obsessional thoughts, do not become distressed by them, and therefore are able to readily ignore them without needing to develop ways of coping with them that are ultimately problematic.

In order to get a sense of how things have changed for you since you began working on overcoming OCD through this book, review where you were with your symptoms when you started and where you are now. Turn back to chapter 2. In Focus Exercises 2.2, 2.4, and 2.5, you rated the extent to which your thoughts were frequent and upsetting, the extent to which you felt your coping strategies were necessary and uncontrollable, and the extent to which you used thought control strategies to manage your thoughts. To get an idea of how far you've progressed, do those three exercises again. If your responses have shifted to the left (that is, toward the 0 to 1 end of the scale), then you have definitely made some gains.

If they have not shifted very much, or not as much as you would like, then you may benefit from continued exposure and the use of thought records, to catch faulty appraisals of the meaning of your obsessional thoughts and to generate a more balanced view of them. It is possible that you need the help of a trained professional, such as a psychologist or psychiatrist. A well-trained therapist can provide a structured treatment plan that is tailored directly to your symptoms and can assist you in overcoming obstacles to treatment. To find a mental-health professional in your area, you can consult your local yellowpages. There are a number of mental-health organizations with Web sites that provide the names of therapists in your general geographic region. These include the following:

- The Obsessive-Compulsive Foundation
  676 State St., New Haven CT 06511
  Ph: (203) 401-2070; Fax (203) 401-2076;
  www.ocfoundation.org

- The Anxiety Disorders Association of America
  8730 Georgia Ave., Suite 600, Silver Spring, MD 20910
  Ph: (240) 485-1001; Fax: (240) 485-1035; www.adaa.org

- The Association for Advancement of Behavior Therapy
  305 Seventh Ave., 16th Floor, New York, NY 10001
  Ph: (212) 647-1890; Fax: (212) 647-1865; www.aabt.org

- The Academy of Cognitive Therapy
  One Belmont Ave., Suite 700, Bala Cynwyd, PA 19004
  Ph: (610) 664-1273; Fax: (610) 664-5137
  www.academyofct.org; E-mail: info@academyofct.org

STRATEGIES FOR MAINTAINING GAINS

To maintain your gains, you first need to continue exposure to the thoughts, situations, places, people, and so on that were on your exposure ladder. Consider Stefan, who was afraid of spiders. If he were to begin avoiding spiders again after treatment, it is likely that his fear of spiders would return, for his experience of not being afraid of spiders is so limited, relative to his experience of being afraid of them. When he sees a spider, he is more likely to remember it as something to be feared rather than as something that is not harmful. So, if you stop exposing yourself to the situations on your exposure ladder, your more recent memory of those situations may well be eclipsed by your older, negative, but greater memories of them.

Second, remember that everyone experiences obsessions from time to time. You, too, will experience obsessions from time to time, some of them more intense than others. In order to maintain your gains, you need to continue responding to the obsessions in the way you learned in this book. That means noticing when an obsession is causing you distress, identifying your appraisal of its meaning, and developing a more balanced, realistic appraisal. It is crucial that you do not start using your old coping strategies in response to the obsession. Some people fall into the trap of experiencing an obsession that can efficiently be resolved by use of checking, reassurance seeking, and so on, and so go for the quick fix by using one of these old strategies. The sense of control and relief they experience is so welcome, they are likely to use such strategies again in response to the obsession, and the idea to endure the obsession without using a problematic coping strategy becomes ever more unattractive. The obsession persists and the formerly efficient coping strategies become less effective. Within weeks, you can be back to having a problem with both persistent obsessions and the need to perform time-consuming compulsions and neutralizing acts.

Thus, a major key to maintaining your gains is to continue to resist all urges to use compulsions, neutralizing, thought control, and avoidance in response to *any* obsessional thought. If you begin to use your old ways of coping with obsessional thoughts, your OCD is likely to get the better of you. One way you can avoid using old strategies is to continue to review the new strategies. Hang on to your focus exercises and this book, and review all the material about once a month or so, even if you are not having a problem with OCD. This will help you remember the important factors in the persistence of your OCD and how to overcome them.

> **If you begin to use your old ways of coping with obsessional thoughts, your OCD is likely to get the better of you.**

MANAGING THE RETURN OF SYMPTOMS

The amount of stress and anxiety you experience in your daily life can have an important impact on your OCD symptoms. Once an anxiety response is triggered (say by a tight work deadline, the impending arrival of a new baby, or an unpleasant performance review), you can become threat sensitive. This means being apt to interpret neutral and benign events in a threatening manner, and becoming reactive to anything that is potentially threatening, such as a negative, unwanted thought. You should expect that your obsessions may return or recur with greater intensity in times of stress. Steketee (1999) distinguishes between a lapse and a relapse. A relapse is a return to full-blown OCD. A lapse is a temporary period of time in which obsessions and urges to engage in old coping strategies return, and is typically a sign that you are enduring other stressors. It is important that you do not assume that the recurrence of obsessions and urges to use old coping strategies signifies a return of OCD, but instead view it as a lapse that you can get under control *before* it becomes a relapse. Remember that to a large extent you have control over preventing a relapse by a) identifying and correcting a faulty appraisal of the meaning of your obsessions, b) exposing yourself to the obsession while refraining from using any of your old coping strategies, and c) managing your stress.

Here is a summary of strategies for maintaining your gains. The first part talks about how to keep your gains. Reread this every once in a while to remind yourself to maintain progress. The second part talks about what to do if you find that your obsessions, compulsions, or neutralizing strategies are starting to return. If this is happening, we advise following all the strategies on this list.

Strategies for Maintaining Gains

1. Continue to expose yourself to all the situations on your exposure ladder on a regular basis.

2. Once a month or so, review all of your focus exercises and refresh your memory about the facts of OCD and how to overcome it.

3. Evaluate your success in terms of *how you manage* an occurrence of an obsession rather than in terms of the frequency of obsessions you have.

4. Reduce the stressors in your life and hone your skills for managing those you cannot reduce.

Strategies for Managing the Return of OCD Symptoms

1. Don't panic. Remember that a return of symptoms does not mean a return of OCD; much of the control over symptom escalation is in your hands.

2. Identify your appraisal of your obsessions and overcome faulty overinterpretation by developing a balanced view; review relevant chapters in this book.

3. Expose yourself to the obsession while refraining from use of all old coping strategies each and every time; resist the urge for the quick fix, no matter how minor or efficient that quick fix seems.

4. Reduce the stressors in your life and hone your skills for managing those you cannot reduce.

COPING WITH STRESS

Since times of stress are times when symptoms may begin to return, it is useful to anticipate when stressors may occur. Steketee (1999) recommends that you develop a list of stressful situations and daily hassles in order to anticipate times when symptoms may return. The next exercise helps you do this.

FOCUS EXERCISE 11.1: IDENTIFYING STRESSORS

This exercise helps you develop a list of situations that may bring on obsessions and the urge to use old coping strategies. Everyone reacts to life events differently, and what might be a stressor for one person might not be for another. As you are developing this list, don't focus on what you think in general terms might be stressors, but instead think about what kinds of events and situations are upsetting for you personally. Keep in mind, as well, that positive events, such as the birth of a baby, a job promotion, or moving to a larger house can be quite stressful. You may not even recognize certain types of events and situations as stressors until long after you have endured them. Here are some different kinds of stressors to get you started. Note that this list is by no means exhaustive but is meant to help you consider all the different kinds of stressors there can be:

Family/Personal Stressors

- large family gatherings (Passover, Christmas, Thanksgiving, Eid)

- illness of a close family member (onset or worsening)

- death of a close friend or family member

- marriage (own or child's), birth of a baby, divorce/separation

- difficulties with spousal relationship, difficulties with children

- financial difficulties

- conflict with friend or family member

- moving, major household renovations/repair

- hectic, rushed daily schedule; competing demands of household and work

■   difficulties with people in or demands of social organizations (committees, charity work, sports team, drama group, choir)

■   religious or racial persecution or ostracization/isolation

■   unsafe neighborhood

■   social isolation

Work Stressors

■   tedious or difficult job, limited autonomy on the job

■   job with substantial responsibility

■   promotion, demotion, or poor performance review

■   threat of job cuts in the workplace

■   difficult boss or manager, conflict with coworkers

■   too much or too little work

■   unpleasant office politics, noisy workplace

■   hectic workplace

■   limited room for advancement, low job satisfaction, low pay

■   unfairness in the workplace; sexual, racial, or other harassment on the job

■   high potential for injury in the workplace

In your notebook, list all of the personal and workplace (if applicable) stressors that you currently are enduring, and ones you anticipate enduring. When you have finished, review your list. Note that if the intensity of any of these stressors changes, or if their number changes, your obsessions may return with greater frequency. What you will want to do in the future is be very aware of the stressors. When your obsessions recur, don't panic; remember that you are enduring a stressor, so your obsessions are increasing in frequency for a while.

STRESS MANAGEMENT

Stress occurs when you anticipate that the demands of a situation exceed your ability to cope with it. There are two ways to reduce stress, then. The first is to reduce the demands of the situation. The second is to develop effective ways of coping with the aspects of the situation you cannot change.

Reducing the Demands of a Situation

The stress in many situations may be created by an unbalanced interpretation of the situation. You may want to use the skills you have learned in this book to identify what thoughts are driving your stress and make sure that they represent a balanced view of the situation. For example, your stress may be driven by such erroneous beliefs as "it is important to please everyone all the time; if I don't, I am a bad person," or "it is selfish to take time for myself or do things according to my own schedule," or "if someone asks me to do something, I should just do it." You need to identify and evaluate such beliefs, reviewing the evidence that supports them and the evidence that does not support them. Your stress may also be driven by placing unrealistic demands on yourself. If you are placing higher demands on yourself than you would a friend in a similar situation, then you may want to consider reducing them. The first step in stress reduction is to make sure that you are not generating stress unnecessarily through an erroneous view of the situation.

Of course there are many situations that are objectively stressful. Sometimes you can reduce stress by changing the situation or your level of involvement in it. For example, you can choose to play in one baseball league rather than two, or you can decline to sit on an executive committee but agree to volunteer at special events. You can choose to

> The first step in stress reduction is to make sure that you are not generating stress unnecessarily through an erroneous view of the situation.

host people in your home every other week rather than every week. If your relationship is a source of stress, consider counseling. Part of making such changes is determining your priorities, so you can identify situations and activities that are generally voluntary but whose costs outweigh their benefits. Another part of making such changes is to look for options, even when you think you are trapped. For example, Kareem lived in a neighborhood in which he and his family faced regular religious intolerance. This was extremely stressful, but he believed that if he moved, he would be giving in to racial intolerance, so he felt very trapped. However, when he weighed the costs versus the benefits of the stress his living situation created, he decided that the cost of fighting religious intolerance in this particular way was not worth it. Kareem then determined that there were many other ways to fight against religious intolerance. He resolved to move to a more accepting neighborhood but to continue his fight by speaking about religious intolerance at local public schools and community events.

We all have situations in our lives that are stressful but that we have no choice but to remain in (such as a stressful workplace or an ill family member). One way of reducing the demands of such situations is to gain more control over them. Even if you cannot control the actual situation, you may be able to control certain aspects of it to make it more manageable for you. For example, if you have a demanding job, you may be able to exert more control over it by scheduling the time you need to complete your most important tasks during the day into your day planner and protecting that time by scheduling other tasks of lesser priority (such as replying to less important voice mail and e-mail messages) around it. When demands are made during this protected time, you can handle it by saying, "I've got a deadline I'm working on right now, but I have some time at 4:00 P.M. to help you with this—would you like to schedule a meeting for then?" If you have an ill family member, you could schedule a regular time when you check in with the person or with the caregiver and reduce the number of calls you accept outside that protected time (barring emergencies). This can be handled by saying, "I am in the middle of something right now. I'm going to be calling tonight and would rather discuss it then, when I'll be able to give the matter my full attention." Similarly, errands for others can be scheduled in advance ("I'll bring

> There are two ways to reduce stress: Reduce the demands
> of the situation, and develop effective ways of coping with
> the aspects of the situation you cannot change.

the books and your housecoat over tomorrow, when I come to pick up the empty water bottle").

Another way of gaining some control over demanding situations is to share the demands by asking people for their help with well-specified tasks ("Mom has two appointments with specialists next Friday. I can take her to the first one, but not the second. I would be grateful if you could take her to the second one"). It can also be helpful to agree to a component of a request rather than to the entire request ("I can't drive over there to get you, but I can pick you up at the train or bus station here"). You will be surprised at how well people will adapt to limits if you are consistent, polite, and firm in setting them.

Stressful situations can also come from how others are treating you. You cannot choose your family and you may have no control over who your coworkers are. You also cannot control how others behave. However, you can set limits with others so that their behavior toward you is less intrusive, upsetting, or inappropriate. For example, suppose a coworker regularly spends more than her/his fair share of time using a piece of equipment you need. The way you handle such a situation can either create or reduce stress. You could work around the coworker as best you can, quietly fuming all the while. However, the added challenge of working around the coworker combined with managing feelings of anger and frustration makes for considerable stress. Often people in this situation end up fuming until the "last straw," then explode with something like, "You don't have any respect for me or my time!" This statement is likely to make the other person defensive ("What do you mean I don't respect your time! Last week I did X, Y, and Z to help you get your deadline met!"). Furthermore, the problem of "you don't respect me" is extremely difficult to solve, and the discussion following such a statement is likely to leave the essential problem unaddressed. Finally, it is possible that the coworker genuinely did not appreciate your need for the equipment (for example, was unaware of the type of project you were working on and your need for its completion). Relations with the coworker then become even more strained and may never truly resolve.

This kind of situation can be managed in a way that reduces stress. The key is to handle it with open, honest communication, and to give the coworker the benefit of the doubt. That is, do not presume that the coworker has a genuine understanding of the impact of his or her behavior on you. Needs that seem obvious to you are often much less obvious to others. It is surprising how often behavior you assume is motivated by callousness or lack of consideration is simply due to lack of understanding; hence the need for open communication. Approach the coworker when you are not angry or upset and objectively explain the *specific* problem (not getting enough time on the piece of equipment) rather than what you perceive to be the general problem (coworker doesn't respect you). Then present what you would like to be done about it ("I am working on project X, and I need to be able to use the computer for three straight hours each day. I've noticed that you also need the computer each day for your project, so I would like to work out a daily schedule to ensure that we both get the amount of time we need"). The benefit of this approach is that the coworker has a clear understanding of the specific problem (your need for access to the computer for a certain number of hours every day), without issues of motives, character, and personality clouding the waters. Solutions can be discussed until you reach a mutually satisfactory arrangement.

Similar strategies can be used with family members whose behavior is problematic. For example, if you have family members who consistently don't let you know whether or not they will be attending a family event and do not contribute to meals when they do come, it may be tempting to handle it by telling them angrily that they take you for granted. As in the work situation, this kind of response identifies a problem that is difficult to solve (being taken for granted) and tends to lead to an activation of hostilities, counter-accusations, and discussion that is generally unproductive. A more effective alternative would be, "If you would like to join us for dinner, I would be grateful if you could bring either a salad or a dessert—your choice—and I'll need to know by Wednesday, so I can plan the meal." This directly addresses the problematic behavior (not providing an R.S.V.P., not contributing to the meal), which is much easier to change than "being taken for granted."

We all have to cope with people who are adept at getting others to take on responsibilities that are really theirs. When this happens to you, you can address it with a similar kind of direct, explicit statement. For example, an appropriate response to an unreasonable request for your assistance is to say politely, "I can't help you with that. I've got some tough deadlines of my own to meet this week." Another strategy is to agree to help with a part of the request ("I can't research the topic for you, but once I've finished up what I'm doing here, I can forward you a list of search terms that I have found helpful"). The key is to give a consistent message and to not give in to pleas. Sounding like a broken record can actually be helpful here. This technique involves replying to the other person's demands with exactly the same message. For example, a coworker may say, "I really need help with this, or I am going to be in trouble." Your reply is, "I can't help you with that. I've got some tough deadlines of my own to meet this week." They reply, "But I can't do it without your help!" You reply, "Yes, I understand. I can't help you with that, I've got some tough deadlines of my own to meet this week."

It is possible that after your open communication regarding the problem, the other person may refuse to acknowledge the problem or participate in a solution ("Well, I need the computer all day for the next week, so you'll have to figure out what you're going to do"; family member fails to follow through with the request and shows up at the family gathering without having told you ahead of time and without a contribution to the meal). You can try being persistent over time by repeating the request over several occasions. It becomes increasingly more difficult to ignore your requests if you are persistent. However, if persistence does not pay off, you may need to generate a solution that does not involve the person (approaching the manager with "I'm having difficulty completing the project on schedule because the computer is in high demand and I can't use it for the time necessary to make the deadline") or accept that this person is not going to behave as you would like, and expect and anticipate it for the future (see below).

Here is a summary of the strategies for reducing the demands of stressful situations that you can change.

Strategies for Reducing the Demands of Stressful Situations

1. Evaluate the thoughts that are driving your stress; is your stress being driven by erroneous beliefs about the situation or by unrealistic demands on yourself?

2. Evaluate your priorities; do the costs of continuing to engage in a stressful situation outweigh the benefits? Do they outweigh the costs of changing the situation? If not, change the situation.

3. If you cannot change the overall situation, identify aspects of the situation you have some control over; there may be more than you think.

4. Take control over stressful situations to the extent you can by the following:

    - Using open, direct, and clear communication to solve problems with others:

        - Focus on the current, specific problem (not what you perceive to be the general problem).

        - Give the other person the benefit of the doubt.

        - Work agreeably toward a solution that is effective for both of you.

        - Be polite but persistent in communicating your message over time and occurrences.

    - Scheduling time for high priority tasks and protecting that time

    - Politely but firmly turning down unreasonable requests, or agreeing to take on only the part of the task that is manageable for you

    - Setting your own limits on the frequency, scheduling, and circumstances of managing others' requests:

- Schedule a specific time when you will check in with others, rather than make yourself consistently available to them.

- Schedule when you will do errands or favors for others, rather than make yourself generally available to do them.

- Try to get the assistance of others in a similar position of responsibility.

5. Remember that you cannot control what people do; you can only tell them what you would like them to do.

Coping With Stressors You Can't Change

If you have limited control over the stressors in your life, it can be very helpful simply to accept them. Acceptance does not mean liking or approving of the conditions that create the stress, but rather acknowledging to yourself that the stressful situation exists and learning to expect it, rather than being taken by surprise and being outraged by it.

Protective Actions

One thing you can do is make sure that you find ways of having regular breaks from the stressor. For example, take your lunch hour instead of working through it, ask others to help you care for an ill or elderly person, and take vacations. Another protective action is to involve yourself in rewarding activities outside the source of stress. The greater the number or quality of rewarding activities you can engage in, the less important any one activity will be in your overall life satisfaction and well-being—assuming, of course, that such activities are engaged in at a level, intensity, and pace that keep them truly rewarding, as opposed to a source of stress themselves.

A third protective action you can take is to create a healthy, positive outlet for your stress. Talking about frustrations with a friend can be a fine way to manage stress as long as it is done in moderation;

however, dwelling on your stress can intensify your feelings of frustration, rather than help you accept the realities of the stressor. Furthermore, if your frustrations are the main topic of your conversation with others, you risk burning out your social support network. Some people cope with work stress by discussing it with their colleagues on break and during the lunch hour. Although it is important to solicit social support for the challenges of the workplace, dwelling on the shortcomings of the job and/or certain coworkers and managers typically leads to a magnification of the problems and absolutely no generation of solutions. Also note that it is during such discussions that rumors are passed into "fact," leading to further misunderstandings in the workplace. A healthier option is to spend your breaks and lunch truly taking a break from work, by sitting outside, taking a walk, reading, and so on. There may be initial pressure to join the group, but this will die down if you are consistent. Physical exercise is an excellent outlet for stress for many people. This can be accomplished on your own (taking a walk or run), through group activities (intramural sports, racket games), or at the gym (aerobics classes, cardio exercises, and weight programs).

Here is a summary of the strategies for reducing the demands of stressors that you can't change.

Strategies for Coping with Stressors You Can't Change

1. Accept the stress; acknowledge it as something that is unlikely to change in the near future and as something you need to live with and adapt to, rather than react against.

2. Expect the situations that cause stress, rather than be surprised and outraged by them.

3. Take protective action against stress:

   ■ Ensure you take regular breaks from the stressor.

   ■ Expand the range and/or quality of rewarding activities you engage in outside the source of stress.

   ■ Find healthy, positive outlets for releasing your stress.

FOCUS EXERCISE 11.2: REDUCING AND MANAGING YOUR STRESS

Review the stressors you identified in Focus Exercise 11.1 and identify the five biggest ones. Write each of the five stressors down in your notebook, one per page. For each stressor, identify what you can do to reduce its severity (by changing the stressor itself or aspects of it) and what you can do to improve your ability to cope with it (by changing how you respond to it). Develop an action plan for making good on each of those suggestions.

Congratulations on getting through the book. We hope that the information we have provided and the recommendations we have given you have been helpful. It takes a lot of courage to make the kind of changes we suggest. It is important for you to remember that courage isn't just being unafraid of something; it also means being afraid of something but facing it anyway.

References

Abramowitz, J., M. Franklin, S. A. Schwartz, and J. M. Furr. 2003. Symptom presentation and outcome of cognitive-behavioral therapy for obsessive-compulsive disorder. *Journal of Consulting and Clinical Psychology* 71:1049-1057.

American Psychiatric Association. 2000. *Diagnostic and Statistical Manual of Mental Disorders*, 4th ed., text revision (DSM-IV-TR). Washington, D.C.: American Psychiatric Association.

Antony, M. M., and R. P. Swinson. 2000. *Phobic Disorders and Panic In Adults: A Guide to Assessment and Treatment*. Washington, D.C.: American Psychological Association.

Baxter, L. R., J. M. Schwartz, K. S. Bergman, M. P. Szuba, B. H. Guze, J. C. Mazziotta, A. Alazraki, C. E. Selin, H. Ferng, P. Munford, and M. E. Phelps. 1992. Caudate glucose metabolic rate changes in both drug and behavior therapy for obsessive-compulsive disorder. *Archives of General Psychiatry* 49:681-689.

Byers, E. S., C. Purdon, and D. A. Clark. 1998. Sexual intrusive thoughts of college students. *The Journal of Sex Research* 35: 359-369.

Ciarrocchi, J. W. 1995. *The Doubting Disease: Help for Scrupulosity and Religious Compulsions*. New York: Paulist Press.

Clark, D. A. 2004. *Cognitive-Behavioral Therapy for OCD*. New York: The Guilford Press.

Foa, E. B., and M. J. Kozak. 1995. DSM-IV field trial: Obsessive-compulsive disorder. *American Journal of Psychiatry* 152:90-96.

Freeston, M. H., and R. Ladouceur. 1997. What do patients do with their obsessive thoughts? *Behaviour Research and Therapy* 35: 335-348.

———. 1999. Exposure and response prevention for obsessive thoughts. *Cognitive and Behavioral Practice* 6:362-383.

Greenberg, D. 1984. Are religious compulsions religious or compulsive? A phenomenological study. *American Journal of Psychotherapy* 38:524-532.

Greenberger, D., and C. Padesky. 1995. *Mind over Mood*. New York: The Guilford Press.

Klinger, E. 1996. The contents of thoughts: Interference as the downside of adaptive normal mechanism in thought flow. In *Cognitive Interference: Theories, Methods, and Findings,* edited by I. G. Sarason, G. R. Pierce, and B. R. Sarason. Mahwah, N.J.: Lawrence Erlbaum Associates.

Marshall, W. L., and C. Langton. Forthcoming. Unwanted thoughts and fantasies experienced by sexual offenders: Their nature, persistence, and treatment. In *Intrusive Thoughts in Clinical Disorders,* edited by D. A. Clark. New York: The Guilford Press.

Morrison, N., and D. Westbrook. 2004. Obsessive-compulsive disorder. In *Oxford Guide to Behavioral Experiments in Cognitive Therapy,* edited by J. Bennett-Levy, G. Butler, M. Fennell, A. Hackmann, M. Mueller, and D. Westbrook. Oxford: Oxford University Press.

Nursi, B. S. 1998. *Words*. Istanbul: Sozler Publications.

Purdon, C., and D. A. Clark. 1993. Obsessive intrusive thoughts in nonclinical subjects. Part I. Content and relation with depressive, anxious, and obsessional symptoms. *Behaviour Research and Therapy* 31:713-720.

Purdon, C., K. Rowa, and M. M. Antony. 2004. Treatment fears in individuals awaiting treatment for obsessive-compulsive disorder.

Paper presented at the Association for Advancement of Behavior Therapy annual meeting, New Orleans.

———. 2005. Thought suppression and its effects on thought frequency, appraisal, and mood state in individuals with obsessive-compulsive disorder. *Behaviour Research and Therapy* 43:93-108.

———. Working paper. Diary records of thought suppression attempts by individuals with obsessive-compulsive disorder.

Rachman, S. J. 1997. A cognitive theory of obsessions. *Behaviour Research and Therapy* 35: 793-802.

———. 2003. *The Treatment of Obsessions*. Oxford: Oxford University Press.

Rachman, S., and R. Shafran. 1999. Cognitive distortions: Thought-action fusion. *Clinical Psychology and Psychotherapy* 6: 80-85.

Rasmussen, S. A., and J. L. Eisen. 1998. The epidemiology and clinical features of obsessive-compulsive disorder. In *Obsessive-Compulsive Disorders: Practical Management,* 3rd ed., edited by M. A. Jenike, L. Baer, and W. E. Minichiello. St. Louis: Mosby.

Rowa, K., C. Purdon, L. Summerfeldt, and M. M. Antony. Forthcoming. Why are some obsessions more upsetting than other? *Behaviour Research and Therapy.*

Salkovskis, P. M. 1985. Obsessional-compulsive problems: A cognitive-behavioural analysis. *Behaviour Research and Therapy* 23:571-583.

———. 1996. Cognitive-behavioral approaches to the understanding of obsessional problems. In *Current Controversies in the Anxiety Disorders,* edited by P. M. Salkovskis and D. M. Clark. New York: The Guilford Press.

———. 1999. Understanding and treating obsessive-compulsive disorder. *Behaviour Research and Therapy* 37: S29-S52.

Steketee, G. 1999. *Overcoming Obsessive-Compulsive Disorder: A Behavioral and Cognitive Protocol for the Treatment of OCD (Therapist Protocol)*. Oakland, Calif.: New Harbinger Publications.

Steketee, G., S. Quay, and K. White. 1991. Religion and guilt in OCD patients. *Journal of Anxiety Disorders* 5:359-367.

Wegner, D. M. 1994a. Ironic processes of mental control. *Psychological Review* 101:34-52.

————. 1994b. *White Bears and Other Unwanted Thoughts: Suppression, Obsession, and the Psychology of Mental Control.* New York: The Guilford Press.

Weisner, W. M., and P. A. Riffel. 1960. Scrupulosity: Religion and obsessive compulsive behavior in children. *American Journal of Psychiatry* 117:314-318.

About the Authors

Dr. Christine Purdon is an Associate Professor in the Department of Psychology at the University of Waterloo. She has been researching OCD since 1990 and has received several early career awards for her work. Dr. Purdon currently holds a Standard Research Grant from the Social Sciences and Humanities Research Council of Canada with Dr. David A. Clark and an Ontario Mental Health Foundation Research Grant, both of which fund research on intrusive thoughts and obsessions. Dr. Purdon has a private practice in which she assesses and treats anxiety and mood problems. She is a member of the Academy of Cognitive Therapy, the Obsessive-Compulsive Foundation, the Association for the Advancement of Behavior Therapy, the Anxiety Disorders Association of America and the British Association of Behavioural and Cognitive Psychotherapies.

Dr. David A. Clark is a Professor in the Department of Psychology, University of New Brunswick, Canada. He received his doctorate from the Institute of Psychiatry, University of London, England. Dr. Clark has published widely on cognitive theory and therapy of depression and obsessive compulsive disorders. His most recent books are *"Cognitive Behavioral Therapy for OCD* and *"Intrusive Thoughts in Clinical Disorders: Theory, Research and Treatment"*. With Aaron T. Beck, Dr. Clark published a new questionnaire measure of OCD called the *Clark-Beck Obsessive Compulsive Inventory* and co-authored *"Scientific Foundations of Cognitive Theory and Therapy of Depression"*. He has received numerous grants to study the cognitive basis of emotional disorders. Dr Clark is a Fellow of the Canadian Psychological Association, a Founding Fellow of the Academy of Cognitive Therapy, and an Associate Editor of *Cognitive Therapy and Research*.

Some Other
New Harbinger Titles

The End of-life Handbook, Item 5112 $15.95

The Mindfulness and Acceptance Workbook for Anxiety, Item 4993 $21.95

A Cancer Patient's Guide to Overcoming Depression and Anxiety, Item 5044 $19.95

Handbook of Clinical Psychopharmacology for Therapists, 5th edition, Item 5358 $55.95

Disarming the Narcissist, Item 5198 $14.95

The ABCs of Human Behavior, Item 5389 $49.95

Rage, Item 4627 $14.95

10 Simple Solutions to Chronic Pain, Item 4825 $12.95

The Estrogen-Depression Connection, Item 4832 $16.95

Helping Your Socially Vulnerable Child, Item 4580 $15.95

Life Planning for Adults with Developmental Disabilities, Item 4511 $19.95

Overcoming Fear of Heights, Item 4566 $14.95

Acceptance & Commitment Therapy for the Treatment of Post-Traumatic Stress Disorder & Trauma-Related Problems, Item 4726 $58.95

But I Didn't Mean That!, Item 4887 $14.95

Calming Your Anxious Mind, 2nd edition, Item 4870 $14.95

10 Simple Solutions for Building Self-Esteem, Item 4955 $12.95

The Dialectical Behavior Therapy Skills Workbook, Item 5136 $21.95

The Family Intervention Guide to Mental Illness, Item 5068 $17.95

Finding Life Beyond Trauma, Item 4979 $19.95

Five Good Minutes at Work, Item 4900 $14.95

It's So Hard to Love You, Item 4962 $14.95

Energy Tapping for Trauma, Item 5013 $17.95

Thoughts & Feelings, 3rd edition, Item 5105 $19.95

Transforming Depression, Item 4917 $12.95

Helping A Child with Nonverbal Learning Disorder, 2nd edition, Item 5266 $15.95

Leave Your Mind Behind, Item 5341 $14.95

Learning ACT, Item 4986 $44.95

ACT for Depression, Item 5099 $42.95

Integrative Treatment for Adult ADHD, Item 5211 $49.95

Freeing the Angry Mind, Item 4380 $14.95

Call **toll free, 1-800-748-6273,** or log on to our online bookstore at **www.newharbinger.com** to order. Have your Visa or Mastercard number ready. Or send a check for the titles you want to New Harbinger Publications, Inc., 5674 Shattuck Ave., Oakland, CA 94609. Include $4.50 for the first book and 75¢ for each additional book, to cover shipping and handling. (California residents please include appropriate sales tax.) Allow two to five weeks for delivery.

Prices subject to change without notice.